~A Workplace Story

Marcus Winn's Moment of Truth

**A new supervisor faces failure
and takes the first steps to
confront his worst enemy.**

Garland C. McWatters, Jr.

Praise for Marcus Winn's Moment of Truth

"In my forty years in the aviation industry I have never seen supervision described so simply and succinctly as in *Marcus Winn's Moment of Truth*. While it is a good read, more importantly, it is a good road map for first time or long term supervisors."

Danny Burgin
Operations Manager, CHC Helicopter
Formerly, Manager of Center Operations, System Operations Control,
American Airlines

"This places lessons learned within a format that causes readers to feel more in touch with concepts and experiences. There is a hunger for 'realness.' Excellent supervisory and leadership skills do not occur through osmosis. Life lessons materialize as we mature through our experiences. The need for self-awareness and insight are well described in *Marcus Winn's Moment of Truth*."

LaShon Ross
Deputy City Manager, Plano, Texas

"A helpful sales tool for aspiring sales managers. It's a real world sales tool that will shorten the time to become a successful sales manager."

Maura Schreier-Fleming
Author of *Real-World Selling for Out-of-this-World Results*

"Focuses on the real issues of leadership. The message is clear, concise, and to the point."

Bill Webb
Principal Consultant, SuPremeHR, LLC

"What a wonderful story! Marcus's stream of consciousness is the best. I think many of us challenge ourselves and have to work through our ego to resolve difficult situations. This is a great text for supervisors, managers, parents, and young adults."

Teri Holle
Director, Business & Industry Services, Autry Technology Center

To Lynda,
who reminded me that
thoughts are things, and
the first step to making things happen
is seeing them in your mind's eye.

~and~

To the many out there who already
wear the name, "Marcus Winn."
I hope I do you honor.

Published by Management You, Inc., Lewisville, TX
contact: mwinnbook@managementyou.com
972/762-3955

ISBN-13: 978-1480264694
ISBN-10: 1480264695

Ordering information: available on Amazon.com and other retailers.
Printed by: CreateSpace

Contents

Preface

Marcus Winn is a fictional character who might seem all too familiar. I have met many Marcus Winns in my years of consulting and training. Marcus represents any supervisor, male or female, who finds entering the ranks of management a more challenging learning curve than expected. Many of the lessons Marcus must learn are relevant to all levels of management, because there is something to learn every day as we continually develop our talents and skills.

I hesitate to give away the story up front; so, I simply invite you to meet Marcus and live with him through a weekend that he did not expect to have. See if you can spot when Marcus Winn realizes how big of a first step he must take to survive as an aspiring supervisor.

Begin.
Garland McWatters

Marcus Winn's Moment of Truth

1
Getaway

The first drops of a looming rain splattered on the windshield of Marcus Winn's Nissan 370-Z as he sped up the Will Rogers turnpike toward Missouri. Marcus blinked twice, snapping out of the trance he had drifted into somewhere back down the road. He glanced at the speedometer needle nudging ninety and jerked his foot off the gas pedal. A shallow sigh fought its way out of Marcus's chest past his clenched jaw. Tension stiffened his body. Marcus rotated his head left, then right, without taking his eyes off the road that was suddenly blanketed by a wind blown downpour. He turned the windshield wipers on high and let the speed settle down to sixty-five. Another sigh. This one deeper and slower, but the tension compressing his body resisted every breath. He couldn't get to his sister's home fast enough. He had to get away.

The water spray trailing from the semi ahead of him only made visibility worse. Usually, Marcus would blow past such a lumbering obstacle, but this time his anxiety backed him off and he slowed even more. The exit to a turnpike gas station and restaurant appeared. Time to de-stress. He lifted his foot off the gas and took the exit ramp.

The words from his supervisor, Erin Morales, still stung him as Marcus pulled into a parking space next to a minivan. Its occupants eyeballed the restaurant's front door, weighing whether to make a dash for it through the deluge. The disappointment in Erin's voice reverberated in Marcus's head each time he replayed that sentence, "We might have overestimated your readiness to take on this promotion." Marcus wasn't even sure what that comment foretold: termination, demotion, or other forms of humiliation. All he knew for certain was that he felt broadsided, betrayed, and angry.

The minivan doors to his left flung open, and a couple in their fifties bolted for the entrance, covering their heads with windbreakers. Marcus sat tight. The wipers repeated their back and forth cadence marking time to the syllables stuck in his head, "o-ver-es-ti-mat-ed . . . o-ver-es-ti-mat-ed . . . o-ver-es-ti-mat-ed . . . o-ver-es-ti-mat-ed . . . o-ver-es-ti-mat-ed." Marcus knew Erin was wrong about him. He had always performed. Results were his calling card, and he would not be thwarted.

An incoming call broke the trance. It was Lauren, his oldest sister. "Hey, Sis. What's up?" Marcus tried to sound upbeat.

"I guess you're still coming up tonight? I haven't heard from you today." Lauren said.

"Yeah. In fact, I was able to get away a little early. I'm waiting out a rain storm here at a restaurant on the turnpike. Should be back on the road soon."

"Well, as usual, the kids are looking forward to seeing their Uncle Mark. Are you still planning to stay until Monday?"

"You can count on it. I need the getaway. I should be there in a couple of hours."

"Need the getaway? Is everything all right? You sound a little distracted."

"Yeah. . . yeah, everything's fine. Give everyone my love."

Marcus ended the call, shut off the engine, and stepped out into the downpour, unprotected.

A slight unexpected chill had blown in with the mid-October rain storm evoking an involuntary shiver from Marcus. It had the effect of a quick slap, yet Marcus took his time getting inside the restaurant. The hostess seated him at a booth next to the windows. Marcus gazed outside. The rain looked as if it would continue for a while. The trance was back.

"I brought you some extra napkins," the hostess said as she placed them directly in front of a drenched Marcus, where a small puddle had quickly formed from rain dripping off his forehead and saturated hair.

"Huh?" Marcus came to. "Oh, yeah. Thanks. I hadn't noticed."

"Brandi will be your server," the hostess informed him and walked away.

Marcus covered the puddle with one napkin and wiped his forehead with the remaining one.

The waitress, who appeared to be in her early twenties approached. "Hi, I'm Brandi. I'll be serving you. Need more napkins?" she offered.

"A couple of more would be nice," Marcus replied. Brandi produced two more she had brought just in case.

"Need more time, or are you ready to order?" Brandi continued.

"Uh," Marcus glanced up at her name tag to confirm her name, "Brandi, how about some hot tea. Herbal, if you have it."

"Sure, no problem." She wrote on the order pad. "Got chamomile and cinnamon apple."

"Chamomile would be fine," Marcus ordered while dabbing up the puddle he had made. "How about a cinnamon roll to go with it."

"You got it."

"And, Brandi, could you heat that roll up, please?"

"No problem," she continued to write as she turned toward the kitchen, "be right up."

The word continued to haunt Marcus. *"Overestimated."* If anything, all the Winn kids had been known for being dependable and performers. He, his oldest sister, Lauren, and their middle sister, Emily, all had graduated high school in the top ten percent of their respective classes. All had received a university degree. Lauren worked from her home providing accounting support to several local enterprises. Emily, four years older than he, was a pharmacist living in Kansas City, and he, Marcus, was a successful engineer at a respected energy technology firm in Tulsa. Performance was in their DNA.

Their father, Andrew, came from a long line of successful engineers. Their mother, Melanie, was an accomplished musician and vocalist who stressed the value of practice, preparation, and performance. From their parents, the Winn children had learned to value education and personal accountability. No one coasted.

Because Marcus was the youngest child, he had two successful sisters for role models. However, being the baby of the family, he did not go without some spoiling, and he would admit that he got away with a little more mischief than did his sisters. Marcus liked seeing the link between his effort and its payoff. If he had to work harder to get the reward faster, he was up to the task. When he won, he believed he deserved it. The new Z he drove was a reward he had recently lavished on himself for the promotion. Neither did Marcus apologize for taking time off when he celebrated a win. Work hard, play hard made perfect sense.

He deeply admired and respected his parents. They were approachable as friends as well as parents. They encouraged him to speak his mind and communicate directly. He spoke the truth as he understood it. He was focused and relentless, setting goals and following through on projects he believed in. He expected his managers to give him clear objectives, then step back and let him make it happen his way. He relished the praise, yet criticism, especially when he was putting out so much effort, came across as harsh and unwarranted. So, when he was offered a promotion after being with the company only four-and-a-half years, Marcus took it as a signal that he was on a fast track to move up. Team supervisor today; project manager in no time at all. My way, right away, worked for him. That's why Erin's criticism cut him to the bone and left him dazed. *I don't understand what has changed*, Marcus thought.

Marcus stared pensively at the dark screen of the phone laying on the table. He picked it up cradling it in his left palm. Instinctively, he pressed the home button with his thumb, and the screen burst alive with application icons. Two more taps—phone, then favorites—and his parent's names popped up ready to be dialed. They had always been there to help him sort through tough or important situations—his dad especially. Marcus consulted with them before accepting the promotion with their enthusiastic support. Marcus reached for the call button. A sheet of rain slapped hard against the window where he was seated, freezing his action. "No," Marcus whispered to himself. He had years of their advice to work with. He finished the thought, "This time I can figure this out on my own." Marcus laid the phone back on the table and turned his attention to the storm outside.

The phone vibrated against the table top. It was a text from Brad, one of the three engineers on his team, "need ur OK 2 release rpt. Erin said u left early again."

Just what I need, Marcus thought. *I'm sure Brad couldn't wait to let everyone know I got an early start on the weekend while they had to stay.*

Brad came to Millennium Energy a couple of months before Marcus. Brad was equally ambitious, but in a different way. He played everything safe and close to the vest. Marcus thought Brad held back while others took all the risk, then he raced in to assert his involvement and be around for the success and recognition. To hear Brad tell it, most good ideas were originally his in some form. But, rather than make decisions that were well within his right, he sought the approval of others first. If things went badly, Brad could always say someone else told him to take action against his better judgment. This text was a case in point. Brad did not need Marcus's approval. The report was Brad's assignment.

The jerk just wants to say I wasn't around when the team needed my support. I'm sure he'll milk this for days. What's this left early again crap? I told everyone. Erin said it was OK.

Brad was a pain for Marcus to deal with. A couple of years older than Marcus, Brad thought he would automatically be promoted when the additional supervisor position was announced. Neither of the other engineers wanted the job. Dan, the team's senior engineer, did not want any additional responsibilities. Sierra, the other engineer, admitted she did not have the energy for the job with two teenagers to care for as a single mom. Marcus was brought over from another of Erin's project teams to take the newly created supervisor position. All Marcus wanted from Brad was for him to do his job, keep his mouth shut, and his attitude to himself.

Marcus punched in his reply, "It's ur report. Do as u plez."

Marcus took his time with the cinnamon roll and two cups of tea. He had just about dried out. A ray of sunlight peeked through and cast itself on the table. Marcus glanced at his watch. Forty minutes had passed. Time to get back on the road. The tab came to

$6.43. Marcus dropped a ten dollar bill on the table and left.

Marcus felt a little more relaxed as he settled into the driver's seat and accelerated to turnpike speed. The rain had moved southeast, but the chill lingered. He wished he could shake the emptiness in the pit of his stomach and the growing sense of vulnerability overtaking him. It just wasn't fair.

When Marcus took the reins of the team in March, he felt his energy and desire to win would set a high bar and motivate everyone. He plunged into the workload, as he always had, putting in fifty to fifty-five hours a week. Not everyone followed suit, however, even though he continually encouraged them to stay focused. At times he wondered why everyone didn't share his sense of urgency and drive for perfection.

His conversation with Erin that morning kept running through his mind, mile after mile. She had enthusiastically supported his promotion. Erin had been with Millennium Energy from its early days, and her opinions carried considerable weight. Marcus believed she was destined for a senior management position. It seemed out of character that Erin spoke to him as if his drive to excel were counterproductive. "Team members seem edgy and uptight, Marcus. They seem to be afraid to take even minimal risks to avoid making mistakes so that you won't criticize them."

Marcus rebutted, "I shouldn't have to coddle them. They're professionals and should be expected to perform."

Erin didn't stop there, "I don't see you interacting much with your team members individually. You seem to be in your own world at their expense."

"They know what's expected. I set definite goals and expect them to deliver," Marcus countered.

Again from Erin, "The techs need your attention, but you aren't available. They get the feeling from you that they aren't important. Frankly, I think they are looking more to Brad for supervision than to you."

> **"Actions have consequences — first rule of life. And the second rule is this: You are the only one responsible for your own actions."**
>
> *~Holly Lisle*
> *American author*

"Brad needs to spend more time doing his own job and less time schmoozing the staff, including you," Marcus blurted.

That's when Erin spoke the phrase that had been burning in his gut, "We might have overestimated your readiness to take on this promotion." Then she set her jaw, and trying to maintain her composure told him, "I know you have Monday off. I think you should leave work now and take time to reflect on this conversation."

So, here he was, on his way for what was supposed to be a relaxing, long weekend with his sister's family. *What in the world does she expect me to reflect on?* Marcus wondered. *Since when is just expecting people to do their jobs unreasonable? I think I'll just try to shake this off, and maybe by Tuesday Erin will realize that she's overreacting to unfounded and unfair complaining.*

2
Welcome home

Two towering oaks bracketed the asphalt driveway, and their branches grew together, creating a natural arbor entryway that greeted guests to the tree lined approach of the Holman homestead. Marcus loved this place. It had been a safe haven for him over the years. Today, he looked forward to it as a place to clear his mind and let the stress fall freely from his body.

Marcus had already planned to spend a long weekend at Lauren's. However, he hadn't planned for this distraction. Lauren met her husband, Jarod, her junior year of college. They married after she graduated and moved to southwest Missouri, near Springfield, where Jarod operated the family business with his dad.

It was the only home Lauren and Jarod had known as a couple. Jarod knew early in life he would one day take over the family business and began his preparation while still a teenager, learning the business from the shop floor up under his father's tutelage. Jarod spoke often of his father's influence and impact on his life and still worked side-by-side with him every day. Marcus could see why Lauren fell so quickly for Jarod. He was made from the same stock as the Winn family with solid midwestern middle class values. The family he and Lauren were growing mirrored the blended cultures of the Holman and Winn family lines.

Marcus maneuvered the Z along the gentle tree-lined S turns that terminated in the circle drive of an expansive three-story house. Jarod had bought the property from a Springfield attorney who needed to unload it quickly about the time he and Lauren were looking for their first home. The acreage that went with it and the private community lake that formed the northern boundary of their property added to the appeal. Friends expressed concern that the young-sters had bitten off more house than they needed as a starter home, but Lauren and Jarod just smiled at each other, because they had already decided it would be the only home they would ever have. They were long term thinkers and could see only a house ulti-mately filled with the laughter of many grandchil-dren, the memories of a lifetime of family gatherings, and plenty of guest rooms for family and friends to visit at will.

Marcus had used Lauren's home as a weekend re-treat during his college years. Here he found the quiet he needed before tough exams where he could focus and remove himself from the distractions of college life. There was a special bench under a particular tree on the shore of the lake where Marcus had spent many hours pouring over the content of his courses preparing for final exams. He always entered the exam room confident that his mind was clear and focused and unhurried. This weekend, he needed that special bench and that particular tree like never before.

As Marcus turned into the circle drive he spotted the face of Andy, his nephew, pressed against the sidelight that bordered the front door. Andy treated him like a superhero. Marcus never shied from the attention Andy and his older sister, Susan, lavished on him when he visited. By the time Marcus shut off the engine, Andy had bounded out the door, down the four steps off the porch, and appeared at the driver's door as Marcus nudged it open.

"Uncle Mark, Uncle Mark, what an awesome car. Sweet! It's even cooler than the pictures. When can we go for a ride? Does it have GPS? Can you watch a DVD in it? Are you really staying 'till Monday? Have you seen the new Spiderman movie?"

Marcus managed to make his way out of the car. "Hey, Andy, my man. Have you grown since Labor Day? You look an inch taller." Andy had hugged Marcus around the waist by this time. "We'll check out the car tomorrow. Think you can handle a bag for me?"

Marcus punched the remote button on his key ring releasing the trunk.

Andy showed signs of being bright for his age beginning about age three when he demonstrated his adeptness with video games. His favorite gadget was the iPad, which he got within weeks of its first release by hounding his parents until they relented. Although it was intended to be shared with the whole family, Andy monopolized it most of the time. He showed talent for drawing, and he loved making all sorts of figures from odds and ends he found around the house.

"Uncle Mark, will your car really do a hundred and fifty-five miles an hour? Have you tried it? I checked it out online." At nine years old, Andy was an endless stream of questions and answers. "Is it hard to learn to drive a stick shift? By the time I'm grown like you, I bet we'll drive hover cars."

"Well, Andy, you might be right about that. When I was your age, we barely had cell phones. Now look at us."

"Welcome, little brother," Lauren stepped onto the porch, holding the front door open, as Marcus and Andy came up the steps. She propped the door against her back and grabbed Marcus around the neck with both arms planting a kiss on his left cheek as he leaned his six-foot frame over slightly.

Andy slipped behind Marcus into the house and up the stairs, "I'll take your bag up to your room, Uncle

Mark."

"He's been hawking the front door for the last hour waiting for you. He's been getting ready for your arrival all week." Lauren followed Marcus into the living room.

"You and Jarod have done a great job as parents. I don't know how you find the energy." Marcus continued into the spacious family room toward the back of the house that opened up like the great room of a lodge. "Where is Susan?" Marcus adored his twelve-year-old niece who was beginning to blossom into a young woman.

"She had dance class after school. Jarod will bring her home when he comes in from work." Lauren moved into the kitchen, "Can I get you something to drink? You started working out yet and laying off the caffeine?" Lauren assumed the answer before she finished the question and reached into the refrigerator for a bottle of spring water and a lemon wedge. She took a glass from the cupboard and put it in front of Marcus, who had taken a seat at the bar between the kitchen and the family room.

"Well," Marcus paused, "at least I'm laying off the caffeine," he confessed.

Lauren was one of the most poised and self-assured women he knew—much like their mother. Lauren stood an elegant, and well proportioned, five-feet eight-inches tall. Her chestnut hair was pulled back in a pony tail, the way she usually wore it around the house, leaving her rich brown eyes fully exposed to take in everything and hide nothing in her expressions. Marcus could tell she sensed his angst but knew better than to press too hard too soon.

"We're glad you are able to stay for the long weekend," she offered. "I know you love this time of year up here. It's supposed to get a little chilly later tonight. That's good for clearing the mind, you know." She dropped her chin and looked up into her brother's brown eyes, and raised her eyebrows as his cue to answer.

"Am I that much of an open book, Sis?"

"Pretty much, Marcus. And, since you don't have a wife, or a girlfriend, and mom and dad are in New England, it's up to your big sister to pry you out of your shell when you start to clam up. So, relax."

Andy appeared next to the bar carrying a folder. "Your stuff is in your room, Uncle Mark. Let's go out on the deck and let me show you what I made for you."

Marcus grabbed his drink, eagerly accepting Andy's invitation. That was close, "Later, Sis," Marcus winked at Lauren and followed Andy out the back door onto the deck.

Visiting his sister was like being at a resort. The original back deck had evolved into a veranda that was open on three sides. The Holmans had improved it little by little into a space where the family could live outdoors until the extremes forced them inside. They had extended the wooden portion with pavers and covered it first with a pitched roof. Later, they added a pergola on all three sides. The entire area was wired with various lighting combinations for the time of year, kind of light, and desired mood. There was a sound system, a variety of furniture and furnishings to give it all the comforts of indoor living, and a magnificent view of the lake surrounded by the towering native oak tree varieties that blocked the western sun and softened the breezes. The manicured lawn extended all the way to a grouping of flower beds and low shrubs that ran parallel to the lake shore. A walking trail followed the shoreline and traversed the property about ten feet from the bank. The trail was a common feature that ran the entire perimeter of the lake through everyone's property. Marcus had both walked and jogged the entire perimeter countless times over the years. It was a paradise. Marcus had spent hours there with family and friends.

Andy knew his uncle's favorite place at the round table looking out toward the lake and set the folder at that chair, then, sat down to his uncle's right. "I drew these so you could take them home with you," Andy scooted as close as he could to Marcus. "Here we are fishing the last time you came up. And this one is us riding in your new car together."

"Andy, these are amazing. All the detail, and the perspective on the car shows a lot of talent for your age. I still can't draw this well. Have you been taking lessons?"

"No, I just try to copy things I like. Sometimes Dad shows me stuff like how to draw angles and shadows. He can draw pretty good, too."

"Yeah, I've seen some of the sketches he did in college. I think he took an art class. Thank you for drawing these for me. I have just the perfect spot for them in my condo."

"Sometimes at night Dad and I draw together at the kitchen table. It's fun because we make up stories about the things we are drawing." Andy looked up at Marcus, a question poked out from behind his eyes, "Uncle Mark, when you have kids, will you still come spend weekends with us?"

"Sure I will." Marcus replied without hesitation and hugged Andy to his side with his right arm that had been propped on the back of Andy's chair. But, what flashed through his mind was the unlikelihood that he would have a family anytime soon. His career occupied center stage, and there was no room in his personal story for any kind of relationship that interfered. He just did not have the time or energy for any distractions right now. The job came first.

"Dad," Andy shouted as Jarod stepped out the back door. "Uncle Mark is here. Did you see his Z out front? Sweet, right?"

"Very sweet, Son," Jarod grinned as Marcus stood up. The two shared a man hug. "Glad you could make it in time for dinner, Marcus," Jarod stepped back so Andy could hug him around the waist. "Lauren said you got an early start today."

"Hey, Son, Mom will have dinner ready soon. Go wash up and let me visit with Uncle Mark for a bit."

"OK, Dad." Andy picked up the folder of drawings, "I'll put these with your stuff, Uncle Mark," and went inside.

Susan charged out the back door, "Uncle Mark!" she exclaimed running up to him and hugging him around the waist. "I didn't think you would get here in time for dinner."

"I was able to leave work early," Marcus explained.

"I'll show you my latest dance pictures later, but I've got to call LaRissa before dinner. I forgot to tell her something at dance," and just as quickly, Susan disappeared inside.

"It doesn't take long for them to get a whole life of their own," Jarod mused as he watched Susan rush back through the door.

Marcus moved to a rattan sofa in the center of the veranda. "I never cease to be amazed at your kids, Jarod. They just seem to have it so together, and this place," Marcus looked around wide-eyed, "I never get enough of this place, even after all these years. It's spectacular as always. You and Lauren have done a magnificent job with everything."

"It's taken years to get it this way, as you know." Jarod sat in a matching rattan arm chair perpendicular to Marcus. "Remember when we moved in? None of this was here," Jarod reminisced, waving his left hand across the expanse of the veranda and following it with his head and back to Marcus's eyes. "I have my eyes on a fireplace right over there in that corner," Jarod nodded toward the location. "We've put it together little by little. I remember the day Lauren and I stepped onto the back deck for the first time and looked out across the yard and toward the lake. We looked at each other and saw the same thing at the same time—the makings of our dream home." Marcus smiled and chuckled as he talked about it, "I remember how crazy excited we were. We talked until nearly midnight that night about what we wanted this place to look like someday. It was so real to us, and we were so clear about what we wanted to create together. And just look around, would you. What we dreamed about over fourteen years ago, has come true."

"Jarod, I don't think I've ever heard you talk about it that way before. You and Lauren have done a great job with this place," Marcus agreed, then continued, "and with Susan and Andy, too."

"Well, I've never thought of it as a job," Jarod

rubbed his chin, then tilted his head to the left and gazed up to the right toward the open beams supporting the veranda's roof. "As I think about it, it's been more of a way of life, a lifestyle we just lived every day." Jarod reengaged Marcus's eyes. "We've worked at it, no doubt, but none of it has ever seemed like work."

"Hey, guys." Lauren stepped out the back door. "Dinner is about ready. It's still very pleasant out here. What do you say we eat outside; so how about setting the table for me?"

As usual, Lauren had prepared a delicious and nutritious meal. Everyone sitting down together for dinner was a tradition at the Holman house. Jarod had insisted because it was how he was brought up. It wasn't possible every evening, but more often than not, the Holmans sat down undisturbed for the twenty to thirty minutes it took for the meal—no phone calls, or watching television, and no texting.

"So, Susan, how was dance class today?" Marcus inquired.

"We're rehearsing some new dances for our winter program. I'll be doing ballet, jazz, and hip-hop numbers. My favorite is the hip-hop," Susan beamed.

"And, there's a different costume to make for every number," Lauren added.

"Yeah, and the funnest part is we get to help with the designs," Susan continued. "Then LaRissa's mom makes the patterns, and we have a couple of weekends when the whole class gets together to work on cutting and sewing them."

"Wouldn't it be easier just to buy them?" Marcus asked.

"Maybe, but I like it when we all get together and everyone is involved. Plus, now that I'm in an older class, the teachers let us help with the choreography. I suggested we include some of the four-year-olds in part of the routine like they are our little sisters, and everyone loved the idea." Susan's eyes grew wider the more she described the routine.

"And, Susie shows me her hip-hop moves," Andy jumped in. "They are fun to do."

"Well, it sounds like you are really into this. Both of you," Marcus pushed his empty dessert plate back. "I guess I'll get my usual ticket for the show. Right?"

"For sure, Uncle Mark," Susie confirmed.

Marcus looked across the table to Lauren, "So, Sis, how do you find the time and energy to keep up with these two, and when do you ever have time for yourself?"

"Oh, I carve out some quiet time during the day. A few minutes here and there." Lauren glanced at each of the children with a smile and twinkle in her eyes. "Being a parent is a way of life. Before Susan was born, Jarod and I did have a little more freedom to come and go at will, but once we started growing our family, our lives fundamentally changed. It wasn't only about us anymore." Lauren paused briefly. Andy saw the opening.

"Uncle Mark, I have a soccer match in the morning. You are coming, right?" Andy asked expectantly.

"Wouldn't miss it. What position are you playing?"

Lauren reasserted herself, "Andy, instead of interrupting, what are you supposed to say?"

Andy dropped his eyes to his plate. He hesitated, "I'm sorry. I'm supposed to say, excuse me," he looked at his mom.

"OK, then, let's start over. I was about to tell Uncle Mark that when Mommy and Daddy became parents, we had to start thinking in a new way about ourselves and what we wanted. Mommy and Daddy promised each other that we would have a home where everyone would be safe and loved." Lauren paused after making he point, "OK, Andy, now it's your turn."

"Excuse me, may I ask Uncle Mark something?" Andy started over.

"Sure you may," Lauren gave permission.

"Uncle Mark, are you going to my soccer match tomorrow?" Andy looked at Marcus, eager to jump back into the conversation.

Marcus repeated, "Wouldn't miss it. What position are you playing?" following Andy's lead.

Andy picked up where he left off, "Mostly I play

forward. The coach moves us around to try different places."

"How's the team doing?"

"Pretty good. No one kicks us around. Our coach keeps it fun, and I'm getting better at dribbling and passing. I'm the second fastest one on the team."

"Sounds like you're having fun."

"More than last year," Andy confessed.

"I remember your dad said you weren't sure you wanted to play this year. What changed your mind?" Marcus inquired.

"I didn't have to go back to the same coach." Andy answered without apology. "Last year

"We all wanted to win every time. His yelling at us didn't help none."

Coach Spears kept griping at us, 'Try harder, try harder. Don't you want to win? You're making me look bad.' Gosh, we all wanted to win every time. His yelling at us didn't help none. It got to where I hated even putting on the uniform." Andy sounded disgusted.

"That could take the fun out of it, all right," Marcus agreed.

"And, he kept pushing his son Luke to be the star of the team. Luke just wasn't that good. I felt sorry for him," Andy added.

"I'm glad you stuck it out."

"Me too. Coach Flores is awesome. She really

shows you how to play better instead of just yelling. She never yells at us."

"Your soccer coach is a girl? I mean, a woman?" Marcus sounded surprised.

"Yeah." Andy obviously didn't expect his uncle's reaction. "So what?"

"Well, I guess I'm just surprised, because I would expect a boys' team to be coached by a man—one of the dads. That's all."

"She played in college. So why can't a girl coach a boys' team? All that counts is that she's good at it. Right?" Andy's eyes challenged Marcus. The question sounded rhetorical.

"Yes, Andy. As usual, you are so right." Marcus conceded with a smile.

*   *   *

Marcus unpacked his bag and tucked Andy's drawings away safely. The guest room in the northeast corner of the second story was Marcus's room away from home. Little by little he had decorated it with some of his personal items and family photos that chronicled the second half of his life. He picked up an 8 x 10 of Lauren's wedding taken in the back yard, where the wedding had been held. Lauren's smile beamed from the picture's center with seventeen-year-old Emily dressed in her bridesmaid gown on Lauren's right, and Marcus, then only thirteen, on her left in his tux. He grinned as he reflected back on how important he thought he was as an usher, showing guests where to sit and taking the arm of all the ladies as he escorted them. Jarod's parents had helped him buy the property a couple of months before the wedding, and Lauren would not hear of having the ceremony any place else.

There were other photos of holidays and birthdays: some with parents; a couple of him adoringly holding Susan and Andy as infants; several from summer stays, and one with Clark Wiggins, his college roommate during his junior and senior years. He thought their friendship bond would last; however, Clark took a job in Oregon, and they had talked only once since.

What was missing from his keepsakes suddenly hit Marcus as more telling than what was there. He had no photos here, or at his Tulsa condo, of him with a girlfriend. Sure, he had dated off and on, but nothing ever gelled into a relationship. He would become interested in someone, but they all seemed to drift away. Beth, Cindy, Denise, Tammy, Jodi, and a couple whose names he couldn't remember. Tammy was the one that kept creeping back into his mind. Occasionally, he thought back to their time together, and he felt like he missed an opportunity with her. When she broke it off officially, she complained that he never seemed to be fully present with her. He was, how did she say it, "Emotionally unavailable and self-absorbed." In his defense, Tammy came along when he was involved in a big project that consumed his energy and extra time. That was it; just bad timing. He heard she had recently married a musician and was expecting. Good for her.

Earlier, Andy seemed to take it for granted that someday his Uncle Mark would have kids of his own. Lauren, on the other hand, reminded him that there was no female influence in his life—no wife or girlfriend—so looking out for Marcus had fallen to her by default as oldest sister. Now, here he was, alone in the quiet Missouri night with one haunting thought, *other than my immediate family, can I point to even one relationship where I could say that someone cared about me, and I cared about them?*

Marcus flipped off the overhead light and stood in the dark looking out the bedroom window toward the lake. The tops of the oaks rustled in the breeze. Marcus opened the window and felt the chill that was starting to grip the night brush his face and wrap his body. He breathed the cool air in deeply, held it, then released it slowly back into the night. Then he repeated the routine three more times, each time closing his eyes as he inhaled and opening them as he exhaled. Deeper, slower, and longer each time.

Maybe I'll sleep with the window open. The air was refreshing, but not enough to clear his thoughts. Erin's admonition from the morning, *"overestimated,"* hollowed out his heart, his suspicion of Brad's malicious intentions gnawed in his gut, and Tammy's parting words, *"Emotionally unavailable and self-absorbed,"* disturbed him. In this place of love and acceptance that had so many times been his getaway, Marcus realized that, when it came to his life at Millennium Energy, he was very much alone.

3
The girl next door

Marcus was up early. The temperature had dipped to an invigorating 50°F, but thanks to his warm nature, Marcus had slept comfortably under a light blanket. His natural body clock awoke him around 5:45 a.m. He lay in bed until 6:00 a.m., then got up and put on workout pants and a long sleeve T-shirt and went downstairs. The house was quiet. An overall good night's sleep had quelled the harsh edginess he felt before retiring, and a cup of hot green tea was just the wakeup friend he needed. Marcus knew how to make himself at home.

He took his brew onto the veranda and settled into his favorite chair facing the lake and propped his feet on the cushioned ottoman. It was still and dark. The only stirring was in his mind. As he drove up the afternoon before, Marcus had considered talking to Lauren about Erin's criticism, but he had held back. For some reason, the fact that Lauren even suspected a problem caused an awkward uneasiness when he was alone with her. Everyone was so proud of his promotion; now, admitting he might be failing was way outside his ego's comfort zone. Marcus was confident that he could figure it out on his own.

Marcus sipped the hot tea thinking back on Susan's exuberance at dinner while describing her dance routines. He reflected on her very first dance recital. At four years old, success was walking out on stage, watching the teacher, and mimicking something that looked remotely like dance steps—not necessarily in time to the music—and walking off the stage without freaking out over all the parents, grandparents, brothers, sisters, and various other family and friends watching. Over the years Susan had developed more skill and poise and, at twelve, was looking more accomplished. He could only imagine how wonderful she would be at eighteen.

What also stuck in his mind was that she got as much out of the interaction with her dance classmates as she did with the act of dancing itself. Maybe that was just a girl thing, he thought. But, no, he had experienced a similar connection with his cross country team in high school. They ran together every day, both challenging and supporting each other to go faster. Their best effort was his junior year when they were state runner up in their class. He remembered how his senior captains challenged the entire team the year before to dedicate themselves to the state championship the following year. They worked out endlessly looking for every advantage to be in the best shape possible for the next season. No coach had to encourage them or yell at them to win. They had winning in them already and came together as a team to give it their best effort. It was the same kind of experience Susan described. His closest friends in high school were the members of his cross country team. Even Andy's new soccer coach seemed to understand that the desire to win was already part of her team's makeup. All she had to do was show them how.

"Morning, Marcus." Jarod made his way down to the veranda and pulled a chair next to Marcus so they could both look out onto the lake. The aroma of Jarod's hazelnut coffee beat him to the spot. "Catching a little quiet time before things get rolling? You looked deep in thought."

"Just thinking about things and enjoying the dawn of a new day. What time is Andy's soccer match?" Marcus fixed his gaze on the still surface of the lake. He did not feel like getting into too deep of a conversation before breakfast.

"Ten. We need to leave around nine-fifteen," Jarod answered, then sat quietly sipping his coffee. Eventually Lauren called them in to breakfast.

*   *   *

Marcus steered his Z through the already crowded parking lot of the recreation complex. Andy had eagerly accepted Marcus's invitation to ride with him to the soccer match. Along the way Andy informed Marcus that he wanted to park where his teammates could see him riding in the new car. So, Marcus yielded to Andy's navigating when they turned in. Andy swaggered out of the car and took his time retrieving his sports bag while several of his friends came over for a first hand look and to hear Andy's account of what a cool car his uncle drove.

"What's it like to be idolized?" Lauren asked as she walked up with the rest of the family from where they had parked a few places down.

"Kind of intimidating, actually," Marcus answered.

The team was already huddled in a semicircle around the coach as the parents gathered on the fringe. Coach Flores was giving the team pre-game instructions before leading them off to a warm-up area. Twelve pair of eyes making up the under ten year-old team were riveted on her. She spoke clearly and confidently, "We've had great practices this week. Your dribbling and passing skills are improving every match. Focus on playing your position and helping your teammates. If you give your best and play your hardest, you will always walk off the field proud regardless of the score. Let's take our warm-up and get ready to have some fun." With that, the team raised hands reaching up to the coach's outstretched hand above theirs and gave a collective shout, "HAWKS!" then jogged to the warm-up area.

The way Coach Flores commanded the players' and parents' attention impressed Marcus immediately. His attention shifted between the action on the field and the Hawks' coach. Her fluid movements wasted no motion or energy. Everything moved in synchronization—even the side to side toss of her pony tail that dangled from the back of her ball cap. She was toned and obviously fit. There was something solid about the way she planted herself on her feet—always perfectly balanced. Even he felt confident and reassured in her presence. He was mesmerized.

The Hawks performed mightily, winning the match 4-2. After a brief celebration and post-game formalities, Coach Flores congratulated each player individually. Then, she sat the team around her and told them how each player contributed to the team's success. Marcus was in awe.

Parents began to gather their players and leave, but not before thanking the coach for her performance. Marcus lingered. Andy was eager to get back to the Z and turned around to see Marcus approaching Coach Flores led by his mother. He heaved a resigned sigh and leaned, arms folded, against the Z's rear quarter panel.

"Coach, I'd like to introduce my brother to you," Lauren had her right arm in Marcus's left and released it as they approached the coach. "May I present Marcus Winn. Marcus this is AnnaMarie Flores."

AnnaMarie extended her right hand, "Pleased to meet you. Just call me Anna." She looked up slightly to meet Marcus's eyes.

"My pleasure, and I enjoyed watching you in action," Marcus could not help but notice her elegantly symmetrical oval face, and deep dark eyes. She wore red garnet earrings and a matching necklace with a three stone cluster. They were a close match to the deep red Hawks uniform jersey she wore with the name "Coach Flores" on the back. He guessed her to be about five-feet six-inches tall. Her grip was firm, but with a softness to it. Suddenly, he wasn't sure what to say next, but managed a question as he released her hand, "Uh, I was wondering if I could ask your secret to coaching nine and ten-year-olds?"

Anna's smile widened, and she gave a surprised chuckle, "My secret? I'm not sure there is one." She paused.

Marcus continued, "I, uh, I just was so taken by how you had their undivided attention. They were so focused and intently tuned into you during the game. I don't think I've seen anything quite like it before."

Anna dropped her glance for a second, then looked back up, her head tilted slightly to the left, "Well, first of all, I'm flattered you noticed. I've played soccer myself since I was a child, and maybe some of the good coaching I had rubbed off." She paused, then continued, "Mostly I realize I'm coaching nine and ten-year-old boys. I accept them for who they are, and I don't try to make pro-prospects out of them when they are just figuring out the game."

"It's tempting to expect too much," Marcus agreed.

"I just want them to know how much fun it is to play hard and get better at something they enjoy doing." She paused momentarily.

"Andy told me how much fun he is having this year," Marcus added.

"Then, I guess I must be doing something right," Anna continued. "Now that I think about it, I guess I look for what they do well naturally and try to fit them into the game to use their natural strengths. Some are faster. Some have good body coordination for their age. I don't worry about what they can't do."

"That's an interesting way to approach it," Marcus said. "And the Hawks won today, so your strategy obviously works."

"Little boys are wired to compete and are naturally motivated to want to win at things. I just try to channel that energy. I guess that's my secret." Anna paused and smiled.

"You've made a difference in Andy's enthusiasm for the game. Thank you for that," Marcus responded.

"Well, Anna," Lauren interrupted, "as you can tell, my little brother is a bit intense himself. I'm trying to encourage him to relax a little this weekend," Lauren slipped her right arm back through Marcus's left—a signal it was time to let Anna go on with her day.

"It was nice to meet you, Marcus," Anna offered her hand again. "I'm glad I finally got to meet Andy's Uncle Mark. Your name comes up frequently during practice."

Marcus felt a rush from her touch, "I'm sure his stories are greatly exaggerated.

"I just look for what they do naturally and try to fit them into the game to use their natural strengths. . . I don't worry about what they can't do."

Hope I get to catch another match before the end of the season."

Anna gave Marcus's hand an extra squeeze, and released it. "I hope so, too. Enjoy the weekend."

Lauren led Marcus toward the parking lot. "Nice girl."

"Yeah," Marcus grinned at Lauren and the obvious intent of her remark, "very nice."

*   *   *

The midday sun had done its job. By noon the temperature had warmed to near 70°F. That walk around the lake looked like a sure deal for Marcus. Lauren had provided a delicious stew for lunch. Marcus added a turkey and Swiss sandwich to go with it.

Susan got the iPad away from Andy long enough

to show Marcus photos of her last dance program. For the first time, Marcus noticed how the muscle tone in her legs and thighs was beginning to develop. As she stretched through her ballet poses, the long lines of her back and arms made her look more like a sixteen-year old than a near teen. *Wow, they grow up fast.* Marcus thought.

"Susan, as I look back over the years since you started dancing, I'm so impressed with how you have improved." Marcus said. "Tell me, what is the number one lesson you have learned in dancing?"

"That's easy, Uncle Mark. Take time to warm up. Stretch before and after working out or performing. Oh yeah, and take your time."

"So, why is that the number one lesson?" Marcus quizzed.

"When I was four I couldn't do any of this. I look at the pictures and can barely remember anything about those days."

"To me it seems like yesterday," Marcus remarked. "I was just thinking how fast you have grown up."

Susan continued, "Anyway, my teacher tells us all the time that our muscles remember. They stretched and got stronger the more we practiced and did harder positions and routines."

"The years of hard work are paying off," Marcus flipped through the photos on the iPad.

"Now, I can tell I'm getting better faster. As Mrs.

Rippetoe says, 'Patience pays,' Uncle Mark."

"You are very wise, my Susan. Very wise." Marcus hugged her tightly. "I'm very proud of you."

By one o'clock lunch had settled, and Marcus was ready for his walk. He changed into his workout clothes and headed out to the trail just a few paces off the lake's southern shore. Which direction: East or West? He decided to head East. The trail wound four and a quarter miles around the perimeter of the lake. Many owners kept slips for boats, but the lake was not really suited for water skiing. Jet skis were a more common sight. There was a beach swimming area near a community center and pool on the north-eastern quadrant. By far, the most common sport on the lake was fishing. Bass and crappie were amply stocked. The trail passed through frequent groves of trees that, by-and-large, were left in their natural state. Only a few owners cleared the undergrowth, and at that, the clearing was kept to areas closest to homes. Since the forest shielded most houses, there was a feeling of being secluded in the wild.

If he walked the entire loop, as he intended, he expected to be gone a couple of hours max. The image of Anna working with her team lingered in Marcus's thoughts as he began. His immediate attraction to her was an unexpected, yet very welcome, distraction. Marcus redirected his focus on Erin's conversation and the still fresh wound to his ego. His intentions as a supervisor were sincere, or so he had convinced himself. He wanted his group to perform at their peak and had fiercely challenged them to do so. The emerging renewable energy market had become suddenly more attractive to investors. Millennium Energy was locked in a race with a competitor to improve technology for generating wind energy. When his part of the project hit a snag three months ago, Marcus gathered his team and challenged them to try harder, even if it meant putting in more time nights and on weekends. They had to win the race to develop a prototype that would attract additional investors. His mind jumped back to a team meeting during that time. Progress was slow. Marcus countered by pushing everyone that much harder. New ideas were not coming. "Come on. Think! Don't you care if we win?" he remembered shouting in a fit of frustration. "You're making me look bad here." Then, he stormed out of the conference room, leaving everyone stunned.

Then, something Andy said last night about his former soccer coach hijacked his thoughts. *"Last year Coach Spears kept griping at us, 'Try harder, try harder. Don't you want to win? You're making me look bad.' Gosh, we all wanted to win every time. His yelling didn't help none. It got to where I hated even putting on the uniform."*

Marcus stopped in his tracks. He heard his own rant anew through Andy's ears. Marcus thought, *could it possibly be that I am a Coach Spears?* And, then he just as quickly dismissed the notion. *Surely not . . . I hope.*

A wind gust fluttered the back of Marcus's cotton T-shirt chilling the perspiration down his back and snapping him out of his trance. He didn't realize he had worked up the sweat and that his heart rate was elevated. He touched the back of his neck and felt the dampness of his hair. He could feel the small sweat beads making their way down toward his collar line. He must have picked up his pace as his mind traced back over the past few months and the tension he had been facing at work. He was back in the moment now, and he just stood there.

The sun cast a lattice work of shadows across the trail mapping the bare intertwined branches over-head. He had covered a little over half a mile without noticing anything about the homes he had passed. Maybe it was because he already knew them so well from years of walking the trail. Most yards were not fenced, but a few had sight barriers of various kinds around back yard pools that kept wandering eyes at bay just in case a sunbather wanted privacy. He did not recall seeing anyone outside. Maybe they were inside watching college football. Usually he kept up with his favorite teams, but that didn't seem as important today. He could see a few boats on the lake: fishing, it looked like. A dog barked in the distance.

Birds chirped and flittered from branch to branch. They couldn't stay perched long. He just listened.

That's when Marcus thought he heard sniffling, or sobbing, or something that sounded like it, but he hadn't met anyone on the trail, and he didn't see anyone coming up from behind when he pivoted about a quarter of a turn to his left to look back down the trail. He stilled himself and listened. There it was again, definitely sobbing. To the right, the underbrush was thin. Nothing there. To his left, the brush was thicker between the lake and the trail, which had taken a turn slightly away from the shoreline and up a small hill. Marcus took three steps up the trail quietly, stopped, and listened again. The sound was toward the water. Marcus positioned himself behind an oak, and, when he heard the sobs again, he peeked around it and surveyed the underbrush between himself and the lake.

A squirrel leapt from the trunk of a nearby hickory tree onto the leafy carpet and scampered through the leaves. The sudden rustle broke the silence startling both Marcus and whoever was concealed nearby. His eyes followed the squirrel through the underbrush to where it darted across the trail ahead. Marcus turned his attention back toward the area between him and the lake, and as he did, he caught a movement about thirty feet off the trail toward the shore mostly obscured by the thicket between them. He took several steps toward the movement when a girl's voice shouted out, "Who's there? Is someone there?"

Marcus didn't know whether to respond or to keep moving quietly up the trail. He could see the girl stand and rub her nose with her shirt sleeve. "I said, is someone there?" She dusted off the bottom of her jeans with both hands. "Johnny, are you spying on me again, you little creep?"

Marcus moved more into the open where he could see the girl better, and where she could see him as well. She spotted Marcus and grabbed for a branch on the ground suitable for a club and readied herself to swing. "Don't come any closer. I warn you. Were you spying on me?"

"Whoa, whoa, whoa just a minute," Marcus raised his hands, palms up and toward the girl. "I was just walking by and thought I heard someone crying, that's all," sounding apologetic.

The girl held her pose and stabilized her stance. "You must of heard the wind. I wasn't crying. Just the sniffles, that's all." She wiped her nose on her shirt sleeve again without dropping the branch.

"Hey, it's cool. I'm not going to hurt you," Marcus assured her lowering his hands slowly and relaxed his stance to show he was not aggressive. The girl's auburn hair fell over her shoulders. It was mussed up on her forehead where she had held her head in her hands. Her eyes were still red and showed recent tears. She sniffled again. "Are you sure you're OK?" Marcus asked, staying his ground.

"What's it to you?" the girl locked her eyes on Marcus, keeping her guard.

"I've been walking this trail since I was a teenager," Marcus broke the eye contact and glanced up and down the trail as he spoke, "I have a quiet place of my own along the shore around on the south shore where I go to get away. Especially when something's troubling me." He paused.

The girl loosened her grip and let the branch rest on her left shoulder. Her body relaxed a bit.

"I'm out for a walk trying to work out some stuff, too." Marcus offered and waited for a response. The girl just took a deep quick breath and let it out slowly, but kept her eyes fixed warily on Marcus. "It's a nice day to sit by the lake and think. I could use some company while I catch my breath and cool down bit," Marcus suggested.

"Promise you'll keep your distance?" the girl quizzed warily and eyed Marcus up and down as if trying to decide for herself.

"Promise," Marcus assured her.

"Well, I guess it would be OK," she granted. "But keep your distance like I said," she warned.

Marcus made his way down the slight incline. The girl dropped the club to her left side and backed up to where she had been sitting next to a tree about six feet from the water's edge. The terrain and exposed tree roots formed a natural seat in the slope. The spot looked like it had been used often for this purpose. The grass was worn down where she sat and rested her feet. Marcus picked a spot a couple of arm's length away and sat down first, facing toward the water but angled so that he could see the girl easily with a slight turn of his head toward the left. The girl followed suit. Marcus noticed she kept the club close at hand.

"My name is Marcus Winn," Marcus took the initiative. "I live in Tulsa, and I'm visiting my sister for the weekend. She lives about half a mile around on the south side."

"Jeannie," was all she offered.

"Who's Johnny?" Marcus asked.

"Why do you ask about Johnny? How do you know about Johnny?" Jeannie was on guard again.

"You shouted the name out a minute ago before you saw me," Marcus reminded.

"Oh. Yeah." Jeannie paused and wiped her nose again on her left sleeve. "He's my creep of a little brother."

"So, what's the deal with him?" Marcus thought there might be an opening to have a conversation.

Jeannie decided it was OK to answer, "He sneaks around and spies on me all the time, then tattles to my parents about stuff. Usually stuff he just makes up."

"Hmm, I see," Marcus sympathized, and added, "I have two older sisters myself. Lauren is my oldest sister by eight years; then, I have another sister who is four years older. Emily is her name. She lives in Kansas City. I'm sure I pestered them too when I was younger."

"It's way more than pestering. Johnny's a nosy little sh-h-h--," Jeannie caught herself in mid word then rephrased, "little jerk." She paused and shook her head side to side, obviously in a momentary reflection, "Gosh, I wish I was an only child."

"How old is he?" Marcus inquired.

"Twelve. He's twelve."

"And you're . . . sixt"

"Eighteen." Jeannie cut in tersely before Marcus could get the number out. "Eighteen. Or at least I will be first week in November," she explained glancing over to Marcus. "OK. Seventeen . . . but old enough to take care of myself," she affirmed, then went quiet and fixed her gaze on the calm surface of the lake. Marcus followed her lead and relaxed his posture, pulling his right knee up toward his chest and resting his right forearm over it. A couple of minutes passed in silence. It seemed longer.

"Have you ever just wanted to shove it all and take off?" Jeannie broke the silence, but kept her pose.

"How do you mean?" Marcus shifted his weight a

little to the left to make eye contact.

"I mean, just pack it up and take off and get away from all the sh-h-h--," she caught herself again, "all the crap."

"Sometimes it feels that way," Marcus admitted. "But I never felt that way when I was a ki--," Marcus stopped before offending her by calling her a kid, "you know, when I was seventeen." Marcus paused, then pressed, "Sounds desperate."

"If you only knew the hell I live in," Jeannie started to tear up. Marcus didn't push. He just listened.

"I feel like . . . I feel like I'm one big inconvenience. That's all, just an inconvenience to my mom and Nick." Jeannie fought back unwanted tears and rubbed her eyes with the heels of her palms. Marcus remained silent and gazed at the lake.

"Jeez, I just hate to wake up most days feeling like I make about as much difference to my mom as one more drop of water in that lake." Jeannie's shoulders heaved from a heavy sigh. "And Nick! Nick gives me the heebie jeebies. The way that slime ball looks at me. I feel like he's undressing me with his eyes behind my back. I swear I can feel him ogling me."

"Your dad?!" Marcus exclaimed incredulously.

"Gosh, no! Nick is my step-dad. My real dad lives in Chicago now," Jeannie explained and continued. "About five years ago we lived outside St. Louis. Dad had a good job. I don't know exactly what he did, but he made decent money. Some kind of manufacturing, I think." Jeannie paused and added, "But Mom spent it all and more on clothes, spas, a new car every couple of years, night clubbing, running with the neighborhood girls trying to keep up with their socializing, and stuff like that. Dad worked, Mom stayed on the go, and I was left mostly to myself. Sometimes with Johnny to look after."

She went on, "Then Dad lost his job all of a sudden. The place he worked closed down. All I remember is some other company bought it, and everybody got laid off. He looked for work, but didn't have any luck. One day I came home from school and met Nick coming out the front door. A week later Dad was gone. He said he was going to Chicago to look for work, and he would come get me and Johnny when he got settled. That hasn't happened. Mom married Nick because he had money. Mostly an inheritance I think, but there's plenty of it. Nick works out of the house, doing what, I don't know. He buys and sells stuff. But, he spends most of his time working in his carpentry shop. Mom gripes at him because she wants to go out with friends, but Nick isn't much for that. They argue a lot. And Johnny is a spoiled brat. Causing me grief is his biggest pleasure." Jeannie got quiet again.

"How did you all end up here?" Marcus was curious.

Jeannie looked Marcus squarely in the eyes, "I have no earthly idea. A couple of years ago Nick just up and told us we were moving to a lake house where we could have some elbow room. He'd got a good deal on it. So, I was yanked away from all my friends, and here we are. It's been tough fitting in and making new friends." She paused. "I'm so freaking lonely." Another pause. "I just want to get out of here and have my own life."

"What about your mom? Sounds like she wouldn't want to leave her friends either." Marcus asked.

"Mom's a social animal. As long as she has money to spend, girl friends are easy to come by for her." Jeannie said, paused, then added in an acrid tone, "She calls it having social skills." She rolled her eyes and gave off a disgusting, "Gawd!"

Without warning a taunt intruded from behind, near the trail, "Jeannie's got a boyfriend. Jeannie's got a boyfriend."

"JOHNNY! YOU LITTLE CREEP!" Jeannie screamed. Her face turned as red as the red plaid flannel shirt she was wearing over a white tube top. A vein in her forehead bulged with the rage. She leapt up and tore out after her brother.

"I'm gonna tell mom you're hanging with an older guy," Johnny yelled back as he darted up the trail. Jeannie lost her footing and slipped short of the trail. Marcus had jumped into action himself and was there to offer a hand.

"See what I mean! See what I mean!" she yelled at Marcus, tearing up again. "YOU LITTLE CREEP!" she screamed in Johnny's direction, this time holding nothing back, and managed to stand up refusing Marcus's help. "I'M GONNA KILL YOU, YOU MISERABLE LITTLE JERK!" Jeannie broke into a trot up the trail. Marcus followed staying about ten feet behind.

In about fifty yards the trail broke out of the trees into an opening. Jeannie turned right into the back yard of a two-story house with a screened back porch. Johnny had already run into the house, and as Marcus came into view, a woman about Jeannie's height and build was about half way between the back door and the trail. She marched toward him glaring and tense, her jaw and stare firmly fixed.

Jeannie was still livid as she approached the woman.

"What have you been up to, you little hussy?" the woman scolded.

"Mom, I was just out sitting by the lake. That's all," Jeannie explained.

Marcus had held back a little, but Jeannie's mom walked toward him. "And who are you, Buster? She's a minor, I'll have you know. I could have you arrested." She jabbed her right index finger in the air at Marcus threatening, "I've a mind to call the cops."

Marcus stopped in his tracks, again raising his hands palms up. "Hey, we were just talking. That's all."

"Mom, calm down," Jeannie interrupted. "He didn't do anything except talk to me. We were just talking. He's from the south shore. His name is Marcus. He was just being nice. He didn't try anything."

Marcus was getting the picture. He couldn't tell if Jeannie's mom was a natural red head, but her hair was colored a bright shade of it. He put her at forty to forty-two. She obviously frequented the tanning bed from the shade and texture of her skin. She looked fit in her light blue designer warm ups. Her eyes were emerald green. Same as Jeannie's. Plenty of bling, too. He wondered if the diamond on her wedding band was real or a cubic zirconia. She was wearing six rings and a gold chain necklace with a single diamond drop, also probably fake. She gave the appearance of having money, but elegance was nowhere to be seen.

"Nick! Nick, get out here and deal with this," she yelled over her shoulder without taking her eyes off Marcus. After about five-seconds, "Nick! I said now!"

Then turning to Jeannie, "You were supposed to tidy up the kitchen, and it's not done yet. The girls are coming over at three to play bridge, and I want the place spotless; so, get your tush in the house. You're running out of time, girl."

Then turning back to Marcus, "Damn, kids these

days. You can't get 'em to do anything. No respect. No sense of responsibility. So, what do you have to say for yourself?"

"Like I said, I was just out for a walk and heard someone crying." Marcus regretted immediately revealing that. "Anyway, we got to talking, that's all. Then Johnny saw us and began taunting Jeannie."

"That's being a man, all right. Blame it on a twelve-year-old."

"What the hell is going on, Kelly?" Nick appeared from out of, what Marcus gathered to be, his carpentry shop next to the house.

Kelly turned slightly to see Nick while keeping an eye on Marcus. "This guy was apparently hitting on Jeannie, according to Johnny. Take care of it. I've got to run to the store to pick up some things for bridge this afternoon." Kelly whipped around and marched resolutely back to the house.

Nick squared around to confront Marcus and protect his turf. He was dressed in jeans and a tight white T-shirt, apparently to show off his developed chest, shoulders, and arms. He was about the same height as his wife and sporting hair plugs.

Marcus took the initiative, "Listen, I'm not looking for trouble. My sister and her husband have lived on this lake for over fourteen years. They are well known. It just looked like your daughter was upset, and we just talked for a few minutes. That's all."

"Her mother and I are just real protective of her." Nick maintained enough distance to look Marcus in the eyes without having to look up. He folded his arms making his biceps flex. "As you can tell, she's a looker, and has a natural way of attracting guys without trying. Especially older ones. Her dad split, and it's up to me to make sure no one takes advantage of her. Get the message?" Nick was firm. "I might have to ground her for this."

"I get it. I didn't intend to stir up any trouble. I hope she's OK that's all." Marcus begged off hoping to disengage quickly and resume his walk. "If it's OK with you, I'll be on my way now."

Marcus backed away slowly maintaining eye contact with Nick until he felt he was an appropriate distance away. He glanced up and saw Jeannie looking out an upstairs window. She waved. Marcus nodded at her and turned to head up the trail north. He had barely taken three steps when he met Johnny face to face standing off to the side, partially hidden by a tree. Marcus stopped in his tracks with a gasp of surprise. Johnny locked eyes with Marcus and gave a gotcha grin and broke for the house in a sprint.

4
A long walk home

Marcus felt dazed from what he had just encountered with Jeannie and her family. *This family is really messed up*, he thought. *What a trip they are.* The last view of Jeannie waving from a second story window burned in his mind. She looked like a princess hoping to be rescued from an evil queen. *Let's not get too dramatic,* Marcus thought.

There was even something unsettling about the property itself that made Marcus uneasy—a repressive negative energy. He intentionally upped his pace to create some distance from that place as well as to make up some of the time he had lost talking with Jeannie. Yet, his mind would not let go of the scene. The shutter. Marcus remembered the shutter on the right side of the window out of which Jeannie looked was crooked. Several slats were dislodged and needed to be repaired. Another imperfection flashed in his mind. The screen fabric on the northwest corner of the porch had torn loose just above the siding. Now that he thought about it, overall, the house had a ragged look to it, like it was wearing out from neglect.

Marcus thought back to that property in years past. He recalled that it had always been kept in impeccable condition. So, he surmised, that over the past couple of years, since this family had moved in, it had been allowed to run down some. *Interesting, since both Nick and Kelly were so into their personal appearance.* Marcus mused. *It wasn't like Nick lacked skills. If he worked with wood, wouldn't it make sense that he would be able to make the repairs necessary to keep the property up?* What a contrast between this family and Lauren's. There was more to this story for sure, but Marcus had his own problems to work out.

There was something else. Something familiar about Johnny, Jeannie's little brother. *Shake it off, Marcus, you're seeing stuff that isn't there,* he thought.

He had stopped again. Up ahead he could make out the community center, which meant he was about a mile up the trail and a quarter of the way around the lake. He had already been gone an hour, so he had to decide whether to turn back at some point or to take the extra time for the walk. He pulled his phone from his pocket and tapped Lauren's name from his favorites list. She picked up after the third ring.

"Hey, Marcus, how's the walk going?" Lauren answered sounding chipper. *Funny, how caller ID has changed the way we answer the phone*, Marcus thought, *Or whether we choose to answer at all.*

"Well, Sis, it's taking a little longer than I thought. I got sidetracked for a while," Marcus explained. "Is there any reason I need to rush back?"

"Not really. Jarod is watching football. The kids are playing with friends. I'm doing a little office work for a client. What sidetracked you?" Lauren inquired.

"Oh, I had an interesting run-in with a family on the east shore about a half mile up the trail. They moved in about two years ago," Marcus didn't want to go into too much detail.

"That's the Tripps," Lauren interrupted. "Did you meet Kelly Tripp?"

"You might say that," Marcus responded. "You're kidding me about the name, right?"

"Why?"

"I was just thinking what a trip that family is," Marcus continued.

"So, you met Kelly, then," Lauren chuckled, sounding amused.

"Actually, I met her daughter first. Jeannie."

"That's a sad story," Lauren paused. "Tragic, almost."

"How do you know Jeannie?" Marcus inquired.

"Jeannie also goes to Susan's dance studio. She's in the oldest class," Lauren explained. "The girl is talented—and gorgeous."

"I can see why you would think that," Marcus replied, trying not to make too much of it, then paused before continuing. "I came across her on the trail sitting by the lake, sobbing. She seemed desperate. I stopped to talk to her. Anyway, there was a misunderstanding provoked by her brother, and the Tripps got the wrong idea about my intentions. There could have been a scene, but I kept my cool. It's sad."

"Well, I can tell you more later," Lauren replied. "Suffice it to say that in the two years Jeannie has been taking lessons at Susan's studio, the Tripps have never been to a single performance," she added.

"Makes me appreciate you and Jarod more, and the way you are involved with your kids," Marcus said.

"Like I said last night. Being a parent is a lifestyle. Some people are just not willing to make that commitment, I guess." Lauren said. "There are times in life when everything fundamentally changes, and you just have to be able to recognize those times and be willing to change with them."

"Well, I think I'm going to make the whole trip around the lake," Marcus decided. "I should be back in less than two hours."

"No hurry, little brother. See you when you get here."

"Later, Sis," Marcus said and hung up.

Marcus glanced at his wrist watch. It showed 2:10 on the black dial. The TAG Heuer Formula 1 watch was the first of his self-congratulatory gifts to celebrate his promotion. Why not? He could afford it—almost. He laid down seven hundred in cash, then put the thousand dollar balance on a credit card. No cheap imitations for him. Marcus pocketed his phone and turned his attention back to the trail.

> "Being a parent is a lifestyle. . . There are times in life when everything changes fundamentally, and you just have to be able to recognize those times and be willing to change with them."

Several years ago Marcus jogged this trail regularly. Running cross country stayed in his blood all through college. At his peak, Marcus could easily cover the four mile circuit in thirty-five to forty minutes, depending on how serious he got. At eighteen he was ripped. At twenty-seven, not so. He doubted he could jog the entire distance now. He hadn't been in any training mode for about three years. The pressures of work had forced him to rearrange his priorities. He had put on a couple of inches around the waist, as well as a few pounds, but he still considered himself fit and reasonably athletic in appearance. He broke into a jog.

The community center came and went as Marcus pushed to keep up the pace. Within five minutes he realized just how out of shape he was. He rounded the corner on the northeast area of the lake and slowed to a walk, then stopped and leaned over placing his hands on his knees, gasping for breath. Was that the best he could do? "Five minutes, and gassed?" he asked out loud to himself in disbelief. He turned around, hands on hips, still gasping, and surveyed his progress. He knew the landmarks. "Jeez, under a half mile!" he gasped to himself again. How could this be? Had he been that inattentive to his physical shape? Was he wearing out from neglect? What else was he missing?

Sweat soaked Marcus's navy blue T-shirt. He looked around for one of the water fountains that had been installed along the trail several years earlier. He spotted one back a few yards next to a playground, and headed toward it. He had his breath back by the time he reached it, and he slurped at the cool stream of well water. Then, holding the faucet with one hand, Marcus cupped water in the other and splashed it on his face.

"Better!" he said to himself and looked up toward the park. It looked like some new features had been added. The playground equipment looked new. There were more benches and tables. Marcus looked to his left in a grove of trees at what looked like a patio with some kind of design in the pavers. *Interesting,* he thought, *think I'll check it out,* and he walked over to it. A sign was posted beside it. Marcus read the inscription to himself.

Labyrinth at the lake

Walk the Labyrinth

The labyrinth has been used for thousands of years to help seekers find the center of their being and purpose. It is a physical experience that will help you use your creativity, intuition, and energy to discover the path to your deepest self.

There is only one way in and one way out. It is not a maze to be solved. It is a path to walk with intent. You will walk a path to the center and back, and along the way, as you enter this sacred space, you may find answers to some of your deepest questions and longings.

Ask your question at the gate. Leave your ego outside the circle. Enter with your mind open and receptive to whatever you hear from within. There are no blind alleys—only the prospect of enlightenment.

Begin.

A gift from the William and Marie Atkins Family Trust.
In loving memory of our son, Capt. Craig Atkins,
who sought purpose and peace in life for all souls.
May you find yours beginning here.
August 18, 1979 - June 3, 2005
KIA seeking to restore peace in Iraq.

Another gust of October wind hit Marcus, refreshing his face still damp from the splash of fountain water. *Why not? It's worth a try,* he thought, as he stepped up to what appeared to be the entry point. The path was laid out in light colored pavers against a deeper red background. The instructions seemed simple enough: think of your question, leave your ego at the door, and follow the path in and back out.

The question. The question. The question. He ruminated. The question. Oh yes, here it is. The question: How do I solve my problem at work with Erin? What do I need to see that I'm obviously not seeing?

Now for the ego part. I'm not quite sure how to leave my ego at the gate, but I guess I'll just try to let my mind go blank while I walk the path. I'll just concentrate on the steps.

Marcus raised his chin, closed his eyes, inhaled deeply and let it out slowly, relaxing the muscles in his neck, shoulders, arms, hands, and back as he did so. He looked down and stepped onto the sandstone colored path with his left foot. "Begin," he whispered to himself.

Follow the yellow brick road. Follow the yellow brick road. Follow the yellow brick road. OK, that's stupid. Stop it. I'm not Dorothy, and this isn't Oz. Why did I think that? Maybe because the bricks are yellow? Sort of. Breathe. Isn't that what meditation experts say? Breathe. Already I feel kinda silly. What if some-

one sees me doing this? They'll think I'm some kind of
zen guy or something. I solve problems with logic and
math, not this do-do-do-do-do la-la-land stuff. EGO!
OK. Ego is me thinking about me, and what I think
others are thinking about me. Stop. Not too fast. I've
already made a couple of turns. I don't think it's supposed to go this fast.

Relax. What did Susan say? Take time to stretch.
OK. Another deep breath. Focus on the path. Continue.
Slowly this time.

Overestimated. Overestimated. Overestimated.
Why does Erin think that? Why can't she see what I'm
dealing with on my team? EGO, again. Stop making it
about me. OK. What if I were seeing it through Erin's
eyes? What would I see? Well, I would see one good
looking, smart, energetic, and competent engineer who
gets results. If I were her, I would have promoted me,
too. EGO. So, she did. She picked me over a couple of
more senior engineers. She probably had to go to bat
for that decision. Hmmmmm. Out on a limb, maybe?
And I accused her of letting Brad schmooze her.
Ummmmm. I could tell she was really pissed. Bad
move, Marcus. Bad move. Maybe she's thinking about
how disappointed she is in the way I've handled
things. Let her down.

I wonder if Lauren and Jarod have ever been disappointed in either Susan or Andy? They're great kids,
but I'm sure they aren't perfect.

And Jeannie is very talented as well as pretty. And her mother doesn't even show enough interest to go to her dance performances? I bet Kelly Tripp has no idea how talented her daughter is. She's too much into herself to notice, all that bling and stuff. Just an inconvenience. That's what Jeannie said. I'm sure having kids is inconvenient. Parenting is a lifestyle. A lifestyle. Everything fundamentally changes. Except for Kelly Tripp. She just wants life to be one big party, just like she was free-and-easy without any kids to tie her down. Life was easier for me before taking over as supervisor. I remember getting up in the morning and going to work, and all I had to worry about was whether I was going to have a good day. No budgets, no personnel problems, no hassle from jealous coworkers. No tech standing around not knowing what to do next. No Brads tattle-telling on me to the higher ups.

JOHNNY! JOHNNY! BRAD IS JOHNNY! That's it! That gotcha grin Johnny flashed at me is just like the way Brad looks at me. I wonder what's behind Johnny's pestering? Well, I was the youngest of three kids. I pestered my sisters. I never meant anything mean, I just wanted their attention. They were doing all kinds of fun stuff, going out and school stuff, and I was stuck at home. I wanted in on the fun. I just wanted them to accept me as an equal. But, I was just a little kid then. Of course, I didn't accept that at the time. Are Johnny and Brad just being kids who want to be noticed? Johnny IS a kid. But, Brad is an adult. He should know better. GROW UP, Brad.

Wonder how I'm doing? Think I'll look up and see where I am. Wow. Way over here. How does this thing end up in the center? It certainly isn't obvious from this vantage point. OK. Just keep going. One step at a time.

One step at a time. Susan said when she started dancing eight years ago that she couldn't do any of the things she's doing now. Where she is today is the product of eight years of working at it every day, week, and year. I remember when I started running. I certainly couldn't compete for a state championship the first day. Heck, I didn't even make the varsity team the first year. Only the top seven runners actually counted toward team points in a meet. I got to run, but the only contribution I could make was placing high enough so that competitors finished behind me. I was called a place holder. I wanted to be more than that, so I practiced harder. I ran this lake every time we came to visit cause I thought if I could circle this lake in under twenty-six minutes I could make the varsity team. I remember the day I timed it in twenty-five minutes and fifty seconds. I was fifteen. But, it took me three years to get there. Three years of gut wrenching running come rain or shine. On the other end, I've let it slip away little by little the past four or five years—like the Tripps letting their house deteriorate. OK, re-

solved. Get back in shape. Starting today.

AnnaMarie Flores. Now she's in shape.

Looks like I've reached the center. I'm still not sure how I got here, but here I am. Now what? Wow. My thoughts are just jumping all over the place. Breathe. Slowly. Close your eyes. Still your mind for a second. Now, turn around and walk back out.

AnnaMarie. That's a good place to start. Boy, she sure seemed to have it together. I wonder what she does? Lauren will know for sure. I'll ask when I get back to the house. One thing I can say is that Lauren has never tried to fix me up. They're only nine-year-old boys, is what Anna said. Not trying to make them pro-prospects. She was focused on the boys. Everyone of them individually, as well as how they were perform-ing as a team. And last year's coach was more con-cerned about how the team made HIM look. What a self-centered jerk! Is that the way I come across to my team? Is that what they think of me? A self-centered jerk? Only worried about how I look? That's a scary thought. And I never apologized or tried to make it right. We did have a breakthrough, but I never took time to celebrate that. I just pushed on to the next is-sue. Not cool, Marcus, not cool.

Focus on what they can do, not on what they can't. Play to their strengths and don't knowingly put them in situations where they might be individually exposed and look bad. Work as a team. Help your teammates.

OK, Marcus. You could do better at that. It would be nice to talk to Anna again.

Why haven't any of my relationships worked? Ego? My ego in the way? All about me, and not thinking about my girlfriend's needs? Like I realized last night, I'm really alone. I didn't intend for it to work out this way. Twenty-seven going on twenty-eight and very alone. Self-absorbed? Is this a pattern?

And, what about clarity? Lauren and Jarod were clear about what they wanted to create as a couple . . . and they have. Looking back, I can see the plan unfolding. They have rules for the kids about homework, chores, personal habits, but they don't harp on them or berate them. Ever! Mental note—quiz Andy and Susan about how they see their parents. Jeannie was not bashful about expressing her opinions about her mom. Interesting how two families living within a few hundred yards of each other can create such different cultures in their homes.

Then, I've seen that in the workplace too. When I first arrived at Millennium Energy there was a supervisor in the turbine project who drove his team out of fear. He berated them. Threatened them. Played favorites, and even played one employee against others. Working for and with him was always a guessing game. It was a happy day in that department when he was let go. It took long enough. He was a sharp contrast to Ted on the blade project, who made supervis-

ing look easy. He had a knack for getting everyone to work together. Kinda like the way Anna makes coaching look easy, now that I think about it. Never thought of it that way. Mental note. Get Anna's number and call her before leaving town Monday. Maybe she's available tomorrow.

Hmmmm. Looks like I'm making good progress on the way out. I've gotta write these thoughts down when I get back.

Look at Lauren and Jarod. They are so clear about what they want and expect, and in some way that seems to be connected to how Andy and Susan act. There's more there. Find out. And Anna focuses on the boys and just seems to understand their nature as nine and ten-year-olds and works within that. Make a note. There's a connection somehow between being people oriented, clear minded, and performance driven. Think about it.

Out already. How much time did that take? Twenty minutes. Just twenty minutes. Some trip.

Marcus turned around and looked back at the labyrinth. He still could not see how the path meandered around to the center and back from his vantage point. He went over and read the plaque again. The phrase "prospect of enlightenment," had a hopeful sound to it. How all those ideas came out and seemed to be connected fascinated him. There must be something to this labyrinth thing.

Well, still two and a half miles to go. Marcus trotted off up the trail heading west around the north shore. He could still make it back by four o'clock if he jogged most of the way. He felt rejuvenated.

Marcus concentrated on the act of jogging. He found he had to consciously hold his pace down to make sure he had enough energy to last the second half of the trail. Otherwise, habit took over and he would push himself as if in a competition. That's what had happened earlier when he became winded within a half-mile. Still at that, he had a tendency to pick up the pace. He wondered how often Anna worked out. No doubt she did from the way she looked and the energy she radiated.

They're just nine-year-old boys. That thought kept going through his mind while he watched the trail immediately in front of him. Mid-afternoon brought more people out on the trail. Marcus yielded to the right as he approached and passed the walkers, many taking dogs out for a stroll. He had entered the area where the land jutted out into the lake forming five finger-looking peninsulas. The trail weaved back and forth, making sharp hairpin turns at the points where kids often fished from the bank.

Anna seems to have an honest expectation for the age of kid she's coaching. True, like Andy said, some coaches want even the younger ones to perform like pros, and that isn't going to happen. When it gets too

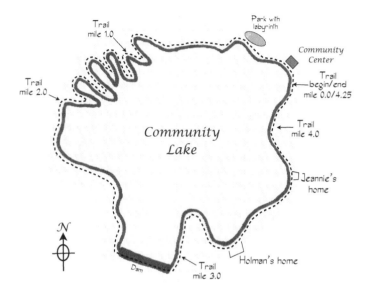

intense it takes all the fun out of playing. Opens the door for a dose of low self-esteem, too, especially if some of the kids just aren't as naturally inclined or coordinated. Maybe I've missed the boat on this with my technicians. I've put a ton of pressure on them to step up, and since they work with three engineers, it could be that I forgot that they don't have advanced engineering degrees. They are hands-on, nuts-and-bolts types. Several are relatively young—like me. Miranda, Sanjar, and Carlos, all under thirty. Miranda took my outburst especially hard. I could tell her eyes were tearing up as I left the room.

Andy said he didn't even want to put his soccer uniform on again, he was so dispirited by the coach. Come to think of it, Lori missed a couple of days work after that. Called in aching with the flu, yet she's one of our most experienced and dependable techs. Wonder if that was just an excuse? Man, I hate to think I drove them away from work. That's not what I intended. Honestly, I was afraid Erin and our VP of R-and-D would think I couldn't handle the challenge. How I would look to them? Ego, again. And, what did I do? Just went back to my office and closed the door . . . and fumed. You're right again, Andy, yelling didn't help at all.

The trail on the western bank ran through the most open terrain. It angled southeast, and Marcus could see Lauren's property diagonally across the lake. This was the area where red-tail hawks were most likely to appear. It was easier to spot a meal in the open fields, but the hawks liked to perch in the upper branches of the tree line. The trail turned back southeast after a ninety-degree right turn. Just after that, there was another hard left turn across the dam on the southern most side of the lake. The dam provided a two-hundred yard straightaway over an asphalted portion of the trail. *Dare I kick?* Marcus thought as he hit the asphalt on the dam. *Try harder! Try harder! Try harder! It's about time I took my own advice.*

"BEGINNNNNNNNNNN," Marcus screamed out as he kicked into an all out run.

5
More to the story

Marcus hit his finish line gasping for air just as a spasm of side stitch hit. "GAWD! that hurts!" Marcus blurted, digging his right fist into the center of the pain under his right rib cage, and pressed hard. He wanted to double over, but stood as straight as he could and forced several deep breaths from his diaphragm until the pain subsided. "It's been a long time since I felt that," Marcus lifted his hands above his head, interlaced his fingers and cupped his palms on his crown. He pushed his elbows back and continued his cool down walk toward Lauren's.

"Hey, Uncle Mark," Andy called out as Marcus turned off the trail and stepped into the back yard. "Come kick the soccer ball with me. See if you can get it away from me," Andy challenged.

"OK, sport." Marcus walked to the center of the yard and faced Andy. He feigned a defensive move, and let Andy get around him.

"Come on, Uncle Mark, you can do better than that," Andy spotted the fake effort.

Andy turned back the other direction and started

his move dribbling the soccer ball. Marcus put up more of a defense this time, but ultimately let Andy get past him again.

"That's more like it, Uncle Mark. You look beat. Have you been working out?" Andy noticed how drenched his uncle's shirt was.

"Yeah, first time in quite a while. Wha'd ya say we just pass the ball back and forth," Marcus suggested.

"Hey, boys," Lauren shouted from the veranda, "you both look like you could use a time out." She raised her hands, holding a glass of lemonade in each.

Andy lost interest in the soccer ball and headed for the veranda. Marcus followed. "Thanks, Mom," Andy said reaching the veranda first.

Lauren sized up Marcus, "Wow. Looks like you got a little heated up on the trail."

"Yeah, a little more than I planned," Marcus sipped the lemonade and moved toward the table where Andy already had taken a seat. "I'll tell you all about it later," he said. Lauren nodded, and went inside. Marcus, remembering his thoughts in the labyrinth, saw an opening to quiz Andy about his perspective of his parents.

"Say, Andy, I was just wondering about something while I was walking around the lake." Marcus removed his ball cap and tossed it in the chair beside him. "May I ask you something?"

"Sure, Uncle Mark. What about?"

"It's kind of personal, and I hope you don't mind my asking," Marcus paused. Andy looked up expectantly. "But, tell me, what's it like to have my sister and your dad as parents?"

Andy looked stumped. Marcus tried to explain. "I mean, uh you know, how do they treat you? Uh, what's it like to live with them every day?" Marcus waited.

"Is this a trick question?" Andy sounded suspicious.

"No, no, no, I'm being honest. I've never had kids, and I was just curious to hear your side. That's all. Just curious. I won't tell anyone," Marcus assured him.

Andy surveyed the side of his lemonade glass, then looked up at his uncle, "They're pretty cool, I guess." Andy stopped there, still unsure about the question.

"OK, that's a start," Marcus said. "What do you mean by pretty cool?"

Andy thought for a few seconds. "Well, we do lots of stuff together—like drawing. And, they help me with school projects. We watch movies together at home. Like, tonight is family night. They take us to movies. We all saw 'Spiderman' together." Andy seemed to run out of ideas.

"OK . . . yeah, those are fun things," Marcus encouraged more.

"They always go to soccer matches, and sometimes watch practice," Andy added. "Oh, and we always do fun things for Halloween. This year we're all dressing up like a vampire family, even Dad. Last year, we were zombies."

Marcus chimed in. "I remember, because I was here and you made sure I had a costume, too. We all went to a party at the community center. That was a blast."

Marcus pressed on, "I'm wondering," Marcus paused, "what rules do you have to keep? Like chores, or keeping your room picked up?"

"Both of those," Andy admitted quickly. "We have bed times on school nights. Susie is always in trouble with that one. She's a night owl."

"Any others?" Marcus continued.

"Does good manners count? Mom's big on that one."

"Manners count."

"Then stuff like, don't interrupt adults. Say, 'excuse me, thank you, you're welcome,' and always ask permission to leave the table." Andy said.

"What's the hardest rule for you to keep?" Marcus asked.

"The hardest?" Andy took a sip of his lemonade while he thought, "Probably keeping my room picked up," Andy admitted.

"Do you ever get in trouble, and get punished?"

Marcus went on.

"Sometimes. Mostly when Susie and I get into a fight. She tries to boss me around too much, and I don't like it," admitted Andy.

"So, what happens then?" Marcus probed.

"I get grounded or can't use my iPad. Once I had to be Susie's slave for a week because I ruined one of her favorite tops when she made me mad. I tore it accidentally."

"How do your mom and dad handle arguments between you and Susie?" Marcus followed up.

Andy thought for a second, "Most of the time they let us tell our side about why we are mad." Andy paused. "You sure have a lot of questions, Uncle Mark."

"Yeah, I'm sorry to be so nosey," Marcus chuckled. "It's just that you and Susan come across to me as really happy, and I was curious about it from your side." Marcus reached over and mussed Andy's hair in a kidding fashion. "Just one more question, please. Do your mom and dad tell you they love you?" Marcus hoped the question didn't go too far.

"All the time." Andy smiled. "One of my favorite things is when Dad comes into my room to tuck me in."

"Why is that?" Marcus asked.

Andy explained, "We always talk about what happened that day and make plans for later."

"I'm sure that is a special time," Andy. "Thanks for telling me all this stuff. Does your mom tuck you in, too?"

"Yeah. Every night." Andy couldn't resist a question of his own. "Uncle Mark, do I get a question, too?"

"I guess that would be fair," Marcus agreed.

"I saw you talking to Coach Flores after the match today. Do you like her?" Andy sounded expectant.

"Yes, she seems very nice." Marcus tried not to sound overly interested.

"I bet she'd like to ride in your Z." Andy added.

Lauren stepped out the back door, "This looks like a serious man-to-man talk going on here. What are you guys plotting?"

"Just trying to remember what it's like being nine years old," Marcus said, looking up at Lauren. Then he turned back to his nephew, "Thanks for the chat, Andy.

"Take your glass inside, Sweetie," Lauren said to Andy as he got up from his chair.

"I'm planning dinner around six-thirty, Marcus. I hope that won't be too late for you," Lauren said.

"That's fine, but before you run back inside, can you fill me in on the Tripps? That was really strange earlier this afternoon. I didn't see that coming. What do you know about Jeannie?" Marcus asked.

Lauren moved toward the rattan chair grouping, and Marcus abandoned his seat at the table and followed. "I'll tell you what I know, which isn't much," Lauren agreed as she settled into the chair and crossed her legs.

"Like I said, we know Jeannie because she dances at Mrs. Rippetoe's studio. She started two years ago when they moved here in the summer. Right away she was a standout in jazz and tap. She's obviously been taking lessons for several years, but not ballet. Mrs. Rippetoe has been working with her to bring her up to speed in ballet, but she started late. I understand that she is well mannered in class and gets along well with all the students, but there's an edginess that comes through occasionally. Last year I offered her a ride home when whoever was supposed to pick her up didn't show. She deflected all inquiries about her family when I tried to have a conversation with her."

Lauren continued, "Jeannie's last name is Irwin. Her brother's, too. Nick Tripp is her step-dad. I've had no interaction with him at all and don't know anything about him. But, Kelly? Kelly, her mother, is a case. I understand that she and Nick have been married about five years. Kelly is all about Kelly, and I don't know any other way to say it. She's totally disengaged from her kids from what I can tell. For example, I bumped into her about a year ago out running errands. Jeannie was with her. I told her we had seen Jeannie at dance performances at the studio, and I complimented her that Jeannie was so talented and that she must be proud of her. She said back to me, in front of Jeannie, mind you, 'She must get that from her no account dad. He was artsie-smartsie, too, but couldn't hold a job.' I was aghast at that comment. Then I said perhaps we would see her at one of the performances, and she said, 'That's Jeannie's thing. I've got better things to do than watch a bunch of little girls prance around in leotards. But, she's into it; so, good for her.' Can you believe it? In front of her daughter? Jeannie's eyes told it all, and my heart just ached for her."

"That's one of the things I love about your family," Marcus said, then clarified. "That you and Jarod are so into everything the kids do and are so supportive of their interests."

"If the kids don't get that from us, where will they go? When we found out that Susan was on the way, Mom told me that children are entrusted to us, and that they would be the source of both our greatest pride and greatest frustration. Just like all three of us were for them," Lauren looked Marcus in the eyes, smiled, took his left hand between hers and squeezed it for a couple of seconds. "Gotta finish getting dinner ready," she released his hand.

"Anything I can do to help?" Marcus offered.

"Yeah, go take a shower," she added and winked.

Lauren left Marcus on the veranda. A chill hit Marcus, but it wasn't from the cooling October evening. Again, something Erin had said Friday morning slammed into his thoughts, *"I don't see you interacting much with your team members individually. You seem to be in your own world at their expense."*

Marcus stared blankly into the sky above the northern horizon. The faces of his team faded in and out as he thought about each one. From Dan, his senior engineer to Carlos, the youngest technician, fresh out of a community college wind energy tech program. Nine people who just wanted to be part of something important. A comment Lauren had just made pushed its way back into his thoughts, *"If the kids don't get that from us, where will they go?"* Then, his mind flashed back to the way Erin looked into his eyes when she told him, *"The techs need your attention, but you aren't available. They get the feeling from you that they aren't important. Frankly, I think they are looking to Brad more for supervision than to you."*

Marcus felt that same tightness that he had felt on his drive up grip his chest. He cleared his dry throat with a forced cough and blinked. He felt an unexpected moistness flush his eyes, blurring his vision slightly. Marcus blinked twice quickly then closed his eyes tightly for a second. He opened his eyes and wiped them dry with his right hand—first the right eye, then the left.

*   *   *

Marcus stood under the pulsating stream of hot water. He backed up so he could tilt his head up and down and change where the water hit from the crown of his head down to the base of the skull and the muscles at the top of his neck and across his shoulders. He silently thanked the plumber who years ago had installed the shower fixture high enough so that a six-footer didn't need to stoop to let the water hit him on the head and face. He could feel his muscles give up their tension to the wet heat.

So many thoughts were drifting through now, and memories of his tantrums and condescending comments to his staff unpacked in a procession of indictments. He had demanded from Sierra, a talented engineer with two teenaged children, that she get her priorities straight when she begged off working later one evening to attend a school function with her son. When she went anyway, he had shunned her for a couple of days. How childish of him. Then there was the time when Chris, his oldest tech, approached him with an idea to solve a testy electrical problem. Marcus saw the brilliance in the solution and hijacked the idea from Chris, taking most of the credit for working out the chinks and downplaying Chris's contribution. The really sad part of it was that the whole team saw through the sham. Self-absorbed. Tammy, his former girlfriend, and Erin were right on.

He had not acted this way before becoming a supervisor, of this he was certain. Otherwise, Erin would not have seen in him whatever she saw, and he would not have been promoted. But, why the shift in behavior? One of Lauren's statements came around again, *"There are times in life when everything fundamentally changes, and you just have to be able to recognize those times and be willing to change with them."*

Marcus turned the water off and stood in the basin of the tub for a few seconds. He lifted his shoulders and dropped them letting his arms dangle to his sides. He made a fist with both hands, then let his fingers relax, then stretched them spreading his fingers as far apart as possible, then relaxed them again. He rolled his head side to side, then tilted it back, then forward letting his chin rest on his neck. *There,* he thought, *take a deep breath, get dried off and write some of these thoughts down before I forget.*

> **"When you are looking in the mirror, you are staring at both the problem, and the solution."**
>
> *~Anonymous*

Marcus finished drying and grooming, then slipped into a fresh pair of workout clothes. He needed paper and a pen. He headed barefoot down the hallway and toward the top of the stairs. Susan was walking through the living area below.

"Susan," Marcus called for her attention.

Susan stopped and looked up, "Uncle Mark. Are you about ready to eat?"

"Just about, but first, do you have some paper and a pen I can use?" He asked as he came down the stairs. Marcus knew where the paper was kept, but he just needed a benign opening to approach Susan.

"Sure. Remember? We keep that stuff down here in the study." Susan acted confused why Marcus would ask. "I'll show you."

Marcus followed. "Susan, I met Johnny Irwin this morning. Isn't he about your age?"

Susan pulled out a drawer in an antique chest located in the study and removed a spiral notebook. She motioned to a cup of pens on the desk. "How do you know Johnny?" Susan looked at Marcus, unsure why he would want to know.

"I don't, really. I just bumped into him on the trail today near his house, and I was wondering about him. I met his sister, Jeannie, first," Marcus explained.

"I thought you and Johnny would be about the same age. I figured you might know him from school," Marcus probed.

"Yes. I have a couple of classes with him. He's kind of a clown." She answered.

"What about that?" Marcus signaled for her to continue.

"Johnny get's in trouble in class a lot, making

wisecracks. He doesn't really take things seriously. He acts a little immature, if you ask me," Susan offered.

"Does he seem . . . mean?" Marcus wasn't sure whether he should use the word, "mean."

"No." Susan paused thoughtfully. "Just annoying." She paused again, seeming to scan her memory for any such behavior, then repeated, "Mostly just annoying."

"I know Jeannie goes to your dance studio. Have you ever heard her talk about Johnny to anyone?" Marcus asked.

"Not really." Susan hesitated before adding, "One time I did hear her

"If they don't get the support from us, where will they go to get it?"

tell some girls that he pesters her, and gets her in trouble with stories he makes up about her and tattles to his mom." Susan continued, "But, don't all little brothers do that to big sisters? Andy annoys me too, and sometimes we have it out."

"I guess that's not unusual," Marcus agreed.

Then Susan offered her insight. "I think Johnny just wants people to notice him, and when he's annoying, everyone notices."

Marcus thought he got the idea. "Thanks for the paper. I bet dinner is ready, and I'm starving." Marcus gestured toward the dining room.

Table talk revolved around the day's activities, including Andy's soccer match. Jarod recapped the college football game and how the Missouri Tigers pulled out a close one. Lauren did some bookkeeping and worked on a project to organize a school fund raiser. Susan had spent the afternoon with a couple of her dance friends listening to music and looking on-line at dance costume ideas. Then, all eyes turned to Marcus and waited. It was his turn.

Marcus was caught a little by surprise. He finished chewing a bite he had just taken, sipped his water, and looked around the table. "What?" he asked trying to act like he didn't know what they expected.

"Come on, Uncle Mark," Susan broke the silence, "we wanna know what you thought?"

"Thought? About what?" Marcus stonewalled, acting like he wasn't picking up on the question. He looked around the table again, all eyes in suspense.

Susan continued rolling her eyes, "Duh. Coach Flores, of course. What did you think of Coach Flores?"

"Now, wait a minute." Marcus tried to avoid the line of questioning, "This isn't fair. I wasn't expecting an ambush, or to get set up."

Everyone waited on Marcus. There was no side-stepping the inquiry.

"OK. OK. I. I, uh. I thought she was, uh, she was very nice," Marcus chose his words, "and I was impressed with how she coached the Hawks." Then he took a sip of water, trying to avoid eye contact.

"That's it?" Susan asked, unwilling to drop the subject, "That's it? All you have to say is she was very nice?" Susan wanted more.

Marcus sensed there was no escaping the topic. "Well, while I was walking today I did think about some things Anna said about the way she coached, and I thought I would like to talk to her some more about it before I go back Monday." Marcus looked at Lauren trying to move the conversation, "You wouldn't happen to have her phone number would you? I thought I might like to give her a call tomorrow."

Marcus tried again to change the subject. "Isn't this family night at the Holman's? What's on the agenda?" Each week a different family member picked a movie or a game to play. No one opted out. That was the family rule. Marcus looked to Jarod with a "get-me-out-of-this-spot" expression. He found no support there.

Finally Lauren spoke, lowering her interlaced fingers on which she had propped her chin while she watched Susan interrogate Marcus, "Well, I wouldn't want to stand in the way of you getting to ask her about her coaching philosophy," she said with a touch of sarcasm, "so, that's why Anna will be joining us for dinner tomorrow evening. She'll be here around 5:30."

"Yea," Susan cheered, "This is so cool."

"*The Incredibles*," Andy added. "It's my turn, and I picked *The Incredibles* movie."

Marcus chuckled as he considered the scheme, rolled his eyes, shook his head side to side, looked around the table and grinned.

* * *

Family night had concluded with everyone retiring to their respective rooms. Marcus sat at the familiar student desk in his bedroom and stared at the blank page in front of him. He had spent countless hours with books and papers strewn across the desk over the years writing term papers and studying for exams. This night, however, he realized he was on perhaps the brink of the most important exam he had ever faced.

Erin had put some tough questions to him, and he was fishing for answers. All he had to work with were

"Focus on what they can do, not on what they can't. Play to their strengths and don't knowingly put them in situations where they might be individually exposed and look bad. Work as a team."

this blank sheet of paper looking up at him, and a flood of thoughts and emotions that he had experienced in the last thirty-six hours. The plaque at the entrance of the labyrinth held a promise he was banking on. If he could remember the words. Something about walking to the center and back and along the way finding answers to some of your deepest questions and longings. He closed his eyes and tried to clear his mind. The question reappeared: *How do I solve my problem at work with Erin? What do I need to see that I'm obviously not seeing?*

Marcus picked up the pen. A gust of the night wind swept in, and he felt its chill hit the back of his neck and head. He whispered to himself, "Begin."

6
A new day

"Uncle Mark? Uncle Mark?" Andy's voice poked timidly through the door along with several knuckle raps on the solid oak surface. "Uncle Mark? You gonna sleep all morning?" The door cracked slightly.

Marcus rolled over from his stomach sleeping position and blinked a couple of times. The alarm clock's dial stared him in the face—9:06. *Hardly all morning*, Marcus thought. Marcus raised so he could see the door. Andy peeked inside, not sure it was OK to enter farther. "Come on in, Andy," Marcus invited.

"Mom just wanted me to check on you. That's all, Uncle Mark," Andy apologized, not quite opening the door all the way, and keeping his feet in the hallway.

"Yeah. OK. I'll be down in a minute," Marcus said.

Marcus had sat up past midnight, lost in thought, and scribbling his notes in the notebook. He stood up and stretched, slipped a sweatshirt over his head, and put on the warm ups he had tossed over the chair before falling into bed. The mental exercise had apparently exhausted him, not to mention a two-mile jog the previous afternoon, and he had slept soundly. He could not recall dreaming or stirring all night. The notebook lay open on the desk. Marcus closed it, picked it up, clipped the pen onto the back cover, and headed downstairs.

"Heard you coming, so I started some water for your tea," Lauren spoke from the kitchen as Marcus rounded the corner. "Didn't know if you would want to go to church with us or not, but I knew you would be hungry. Could you handle some pancakes?"

"Sounds great, Sis, but hey, let me make them. You've been waiting on me hand and foot," Marcus walked over and gave her a hug. "Thought I would spend some quite time out by the lake this morning, if you don't mind." Marcus leaned against the kitchen bar. "So, you're hoping to fix me up with Coach Flores, huh?"

"More of catalyst than a matchmaker is how I like to think of it," Lauren rationalized.

"So, what have you told her about me?" Marcus wanted to know.

"Not me!" Lauren raised her palms like she was backing off. "It's your nephew who is the culprit. Coach Flores approached me a couple of weeks ago wanting to know who this Uncle Mark is. Andy sings your praises making you sound like some superhero. I told her you were planning this trip up."

"So, Andy wants to set me up with Coach Flores?" Marcus asked.

"No, I doubt Andy intends anything, but forces are at work in the universe that are larger than any of us. So, I thought why not seize the moment and let nature take its course. We are only accidental accomplices in the grand scheme of things," Lauren sounded philosophical.

Marcus finished brewing the tea and squeezed the last drops from the tea bag. "What else can you tell me about Anna?" Marcus began assembling the ingredients to make his pancakes.

"Not much. She's new to this area. She is a new associate at a law firm. She got an athletic scholarship at Texas A&M to play soccer. Then she went to law school at Missouri. Graduated last spring, passed the bar and is working at her first job as an attorney." Lauren paused. "Oh, yes, she has become Andy's second most admired real live superhero, right behind you." Lauren paused again, topped off her coffee and gave Marcus an encouraging pat on his bottom, "No pressure, little brother. No pressure." Lauren picked up her coffee cup, "I better make sure the kids are getting ready."

Right. No pressure. Marcus thought. *Why should I be under any more pressure today?*

Marcus finished the pancakes, cleaned the kitchen, and brewed another cup of tea. This time he poured it into a thermal cup, picked up the notebook and headed toward his favorite bench and tree. The temperature was about the same as yesterday, so he decided against a jacket. On second thought, he would be exposed by the water facing north, so, just in case, he grabbed one of Jarod's windbreakers hanging on the coat rack by the back door. The sun seemed brighter today.

People were already on the trail so, there might be a distraction or two. The bench was one of the first pieces of lawn furniture placed by Jarod on the property. Like Marcus, Jarod sought his quiet time by the lake, and he had created a little escape with some shrubbery strategically placed around the bench to provide an extra measure of privacy on the flanks. However, passersby could look over and see as they passed. Marcus walked out to the shore. The lake surface was glassy smooth. There was only the breath of a breeze. He took in the quiet for a moment, then retreated to the bench.

Marcus sipped his tea, then balanced the thermos on a flat rock that served as a side table, and opened the notebook. *Let's have a look at what I wrote last night.*

Supervising! tougher than I thought.
Maybe Erin is right. Overestimated
readiness. Me too??

Self-absorbed? Reality check, Marcus.
The evidence speaks.
Lauren: fundamental changes. Must be able
to recognize and willing to accept. So
what's the fundamental change for me?
How has my life changed since becoming a
supervisor?

- Less time to myself! for sure. people
  won't leave me alone.
- Afraid staff will screw things up. gotta
  watch them constantly.
- Always thinking about work. NO
  MENTAL RELIEF. EVER!!!
- Expected to mediate squabbles between
  employees. Why can't they just act like
  adults? Hate this part.
- People watching every move I make!
  especially staff, and ESPECIALLY
  BRAD.
- Need my approval. regularly.
- Intrusion into my personal time.

FLASH!!! SOUNDS A LOT LIKE BEING A PARENT, Marcus! WOW. BEING A SUPERVISOR AND BEING A PARENT HAVE A LOT IN COMMON.

Connect the dots, Marcus. Compare Lauren/Jarod with Tripp family. Good parents produce good kids (usually). Bad parents produce messed up kids (more than likely).

Remember lousy supervisor in turbine project = unhappy and demotivated staff. Cheered when he was fired. Good supervisor in blade project = productive staff. Anna = motivated and admiring team having fun. AND WINNING!

Jeannie wants out too. Away from her mom and Nick because she feels devalued. Andy demotivated last year because coach more interested in himself. Ego.

ANOTHER FLASH!!!! THE WAY I
PERSONALLY TREAT PEOPLE ON MY
TEAM WILL EITHER MOTIVATE OR
DEMOTIVATE THEM TO PERFORM. THE
TEAM LEADER IS IN CHARGE OF THE
ENVIRONMENT.

Think of Lauren and Jarod as "supervisors"
of the family. What impresses me about
how they lead?

- ~~Kids~~. EVERYONE is respected and loved.
  People matter, relationships matter,
  people oriented.
- Know what they expect and want from
  kids and selves. Clear plans and
  expectations. clear minded.
- Expect kids to do what's right. Hold
  them accountable when they don't, but
  not harsh or unfair. performance
  focused. More than focused—
  performance driven.

What else? What else?

Everyone wants to feel like they matter.
Jeannie feels like she doesn't matter.
Johnny seeking attention—most likely. Even
Brad??
Anna: Teamwork. Help the team. Focus on
abilities not what people can't do.

BLINDING FLASH!! PEOPLE NATURALLY
MOTIVATED TO BE SUCCESSFUL.
EVERYONE ALREADY WANTS TO WIN!
IT'S A NATURAL FORCE.

Anna again: Tell everyone how they
contributed to the team's success. Make
them all feel like they count and make a
difference. (This girl gets more attractive
to me the more I think about her.)
5:30, AnnaMarie Flores.

Stretch. Thanks Susie for that. Take time to stretch. Little by little, then get better faster, but small steps first.

OK — let's summarize. Make some sense out of this jumble.
Start at the top. Big idea!

 "SUPERVISING IS NOT A JOB, IT'S A LIFESTYLE."
So, what about that? What's the big picture? What are supervisors supposed to do? Win? too narrow. make profits? yes, but still too narrow. And no obvious payoff for employees other than paycheck. Help everyone get along? that too, but too mushy. more than a social worker.

Value? That's it. VALUE. Supervisors help everyone create value whatever that means to the individual. Value is profits for

owners. Value is good feelings. Value is
personal satisfaction. Value is a paycheck,
Value is recognition for doing a good job.
Value is opportunity to learn and be
promoted. Different strokes for different
folks. That can work. VALUE it is!

SUPERVISING IS A LIFESTYLE, NOT A
JOB.

ITS FOCUS IS TO CREATE VALUE FOR
EVERYONE INVOLVED.

SUCCESSFUL SUPERVISORS MUST BE:

1. PEOPLE-ORIENTED
2. CLEAR-MINDED
3. PERFORMANCE-DRIVEN

Other principles to think about:

- Everyone seeks personal meaning and
  value (see above)
- Everyone matters and everything is
  personal.
- One big team. We all live in relationships
  (good or bad)

- *Everyone must be held personally accountable. In spite of everything, we still make choices. (Really hard sometimes)*

I'm sure there is more, but my brain is mush.

No wonder I slept like a rock. That's some heavy stuff, Marcus thought.

A familiar, but calmer, voice invaded Marcus's trance, "It's my turn to find you in the trees." Marcus looked up with a start. "At least you're not crying." Jeannie stood on the trail looking at him sitting there. She looked and sounded more relaxed than when they first met.

"Whatcha working on?" Jeannie glanced at the notebook in Marcus's lap sounding playful, "Your life story?"

"At least the last three days of it," Marcus smiled.

"How does it end?" Jeannie continued the theme.

"Happily ever after, I hope," Marcus replied.

"Don't we all?" Jeannie took a step closer. "You look like you could use a friend, too."

"Why do you say that?" Marcus asked.

"Yesterday you said you have a quiet place where you went to sort things out. This looks like that kind of a place." She glanced up and down the trail. "Besides, I stood here for several seconds watching you. You looked like you were lost in space or something. And, you had that squinty expression like you were thinking hard, sorting things out." Jeannie said.

"You're quite observant." Marcus gestured to the bench. "Be my guest."

"Am I in your story?" Jeannie inquired.

"Yeah. Sort of. Yes, yes you are, as a matter of fact," Marcus turned more toward her on the bench. Jeannie's hair presented more of a red tinge today. Without tears, Marcus could see how green her eyes were. A hint of freckles dusted her face, but not overly so. As Lauren said—gorgeous, with a girl-next-door innocence that pulled you in. *If she were my daughter, I'd be protective, too*, Marcus thought as Jeannie got comfortable on the bench.

"Tell me," Jeannie demanded.

Marcus wondered how direct he should be. "Hmmm, what grabbed me yesterday was how you said that you feel like an inconvenience to your mom, like you don't matter to her, and I was thinking how sad that is," Marcus admitted.

"Well, it's just something that I've learned to accept," Jeannie looked down at her hands folded in her lap. Her tone became more serious and introspective.

"Do you wish you could run away, too?" Her eyes stayed fixed on her hands.

Marcus sighed deeply and ran the fingers of his left-hand through his hair front to back before answering, "Not run away. Just figure out what my way is."

"Maybe that's what I really mean," Jeannie looked up to meet Marcus's eyes. "I want to get on with my life, which means getting away from Mom and Nick." Jeannie lapsed into silence for a few seconds. "I really miss being with my dad. He told me to stay with my mom because he can't take care of me right now. So, I'm biding my time." She hesitated a couple of seconds before going on, "But, I have a plan."

"And, what's that? If I may ask," Marcus continued.

"I want to finish high school for sure. By then I'll be eighteen—and legal. Let's just say, I plan to bolt and put my dancing talents to good use. That's all I'll say about it," Jeannie said. "At least one thing my mom showed me is how to make the most of my looks."

"I have the feeling there's more to you than that. Have you thought about going to college?" Marcus asked.

"College!" Jeannie exclaimed incredulously. "Not in my immediate plans."

"Why not?" Marcus pushed.

"Listen. I've survived my mom by accepting the fact that she made the best use of her one talent, which is using her looks to hook a man with money and somehow hold on to him. When I see the world through her eyes, I at least get it. So I let it be as it is. That's how I choke back her ridicule and neglect. I live in the now and the real world . . . And I deal with it, no matter what the ugly truth." Jeannie's hurt and anger flared in her eyes and tone of voice. "Aren't we all just trying to make it, Marcus? Look around! People are just trying to make it, and make sense of it all in their own way."

Marcus found Jeannie's words honest and direct. "Yeah, I can get that."

"What about you? What are you trying to make work?" Jeannie redirected the conversation.

"Me?" Marcus hesitated. Now for his ugly truth. He cleared his throat, looked directly into Jeannie's green eyes, and confessed, "I've, uh, realized my boss was right when she told me Friday that I might have screwed up my job by being so self-absorbed and egotistical." He glanced away, then back. "In short, Jeannie, I have treated my employees much like your mother has treated you. And, I'm thinking they want to run away, too."

Jeannie held the gaze with Marcus for a few seconds before speaking. "I have a feeling there's more to you than that."

Jeannie took the notebook from Marcus's lap and unclipped the pen from the pages where it had been secured. She wrote in it, closed the cover, and handed it back to Marcus. "I predict your story will have a happy ending," she said. "I've gotta get back." With that Jeannie smiled, stood up, and broke into a trot back toward her house.

Marcus watched her disappear around the first bend, "May you live happily ever after, too, Jeannie Irwin," Marcus whispered.

Marcus opened the notebook. Jeannie had written:

Thanks for making me feel important in your life. Jeannie Irwin.

It's a new day. jidances@mzplace.net.

text me 417-555-3103

Then Marcus turned to the end of his notes and added to the list of other principles,

- Understand others through their own eyes, not yours
- Own up to your truth, good—bad—and ugly.

Marcus sat motionless. He stared into the empty space between the surface of the water and the reflection of clouds just beneath it. *Own up to your truth,* he thought. *This is the first time I've actually said it—either to myself or aloud. It had never crossed my mind before this weekend that I was my own worst problem. I wonder how many others there are out there like me? Other managers and supervisors who mistreat and malign their employees, even unintentionally, CLUELESS that THEY, THEMSELVES, are the PROBLEM!*

Marcus flipped over to Jeannie's note and read it again, then once more. In it he saw hope for himself after all, "Yes, Jeannie Irwin, it is a new day," He choked on the words, but forced them out, "So, let's begin." A tear hit the page, then another, and Marcus realized he was on the verge of sobbing.

7
A new attitude

Marcus stood in front of a framed quote hanging in the bedroom. It read, *"The journey of a thousand miles must begin with a single step."* It was attributed to Lao Tzu, the Chinese philosopher. Marcus had heard the quote many times from motivational speakers and sports coaches. It had been especially significant to him as a youth when he began his cross country training. He challenged himself with many first steps. The first step out of bed every morning, the first step of a work out, the first step of a race, the first step of an assignment. Nothing happened without a first step. Then, every step after that was a first step, the next first step.

He remembered how in tune to his body he had become as a runner. He knew at every step of the race how his body was responding, and that helped him to calibrate his pace and breathing so that he would have the right energy at the right time to compete for the finish line—the kick. Running had trained him to be in the moment. Jeannie had reminded him of that. "I live in the now and the real world. And I deal with it, no matter what the ugly truth."

Another principle hit Marcus, and he quickly wrote it in the notebook before it escaped.

· *Be present. Take action now. Now is what counts. Hold yourself accountable. It's more important to do, than to intend.*

Another quote faded into awareness. *"Do or do not. There is no try."* Yeah, straight out of *Star Wars*, from Yoda, the fictional Jedi master. And another quote popularized by the *Apollo 13* movie, *"Failure is not an option."*

Marcus could feel the energy surge as he put on fresh clothes after his late morning shower. The emotional purge he had experienced after Jeannie parted had released a mountain of the stress he had been feeling, and a moment of clarity had replaced it. He felt confident and reassured. He knew what he must do.

* * *

Pro football was a Sunday afternoon ritual for Jarod. Marcus joined him in the family room. Jarod was the closest thing to a brother he had known, and he enjoyed his guy time with him. He also admired Jarod's self-assured strength and understood why his dad felt no angst about releasing control of the family business to him, which was scheduled to be completed by Jarod's fortieth birthday. Marcus had never tapped this reserve of professional advice, but thought this might be a good time to ask some questions before they got involved in a game.

"Jarod, may I talk shop with you for a minute before the game starts?" Marcus began.

"Sure. What's on your mind?" Jarod perked up.

"I'm just interested in your insights as a business executive, and as someone who has seen it all growing up in your family business. Tell me, when you think back over the managers and supervisors you have known, what sets the good ones apart from the bad ones?" Marcus sounded serious.

"Whew," Jarod sounded through pursed lips as his eyes narrowed in thought. "That's a big question, Marcus." Jarod shifted his weight in the leather recliner, then started deliberately, "I guess I would say that what I've noticed as a common thread in our most effective supervisors is that they realize they are only as good a supervisor as the results their team gets. And, to go along with that, they are able to bring out the best of what each individual in their work group has to offer."

"So, how did they do that?" Marcus wanted to know.

"I can't say there is any one right way to do that." Jarod admitted. "I remember how I struggled with my first supervisory position. Being the owner's son, I guess I put some extra pressure on myself to always be right. I thought I was supposed to have all the right answers. Come to find out, it was just my misplaced ego playing with my mind. What turned me around was coming to the realization that I had to spend more time thinking about the effectiveness of the entire group instead of how I thought I was supposed to look to everyone."

> **"Our most effective supervisors realize they are only as good as the results their team gets."**

"I guess that makes sense," Marcus replied sounding reflective.

"Of course, I had some good coaches along the way, and I was willing to learn from them. Plus, I went to seminars and read books at times," Jarod added. "Why do you ask?"

"Well, I'm new at this supervisor position myself, and I'm just wanting to do my best," Marcus said, then went on, "On another subject," Marcus hesitated. "On another subject, you know how much I love Susan and Andy, and how much I admire the kind of parents you and Lauren are, but I'm curious if you ever get frustrated with them or angry at them?" Marcus inquired.

Jarod erupted in laughter, "Ha-ha-ha-ha-ha-ha.

Ha-a-a-a-a ha-ha-ha!" He composed himself, "You're kidding, right?" speaking over a chuckle of delight. He looked gleefully at Marcus. "Marcus. There are times we get so put out with them, we wonder why we ever thought we wanted children," Jarod admitted.

Lauren walked over from the kitchen. "What's that all about?" she asked referring to Jarod's outburst of laughter.

"Oh, Marcus just asked me if the kids ever frustrate us or tick us off," Jarod explained.

"Oh my goodness, yes! All the time, little brother." Lauren agreed.

"So there are times they make you mad." Marcus clarified.

"Oh, yeah." Lauren said and Jarod nodded his agreement.

"Sometimes you get frustrated dealing with them?" Marcus pressed.

"Oh, yeah. Frequently," Jarod was emphatic.

"And, I guess they misbehave?"

"Repeatedly," Jarod didn't hesitate.

"And, they pester you for stuff?"

"Daily!" Jarod replied.

"Relentlessly," Lauren added. "I swear, they try to grind us down. If they decide to work us, they tag team us. It can be a test of wills."

"So how do you pull it off?" Marcus felt he was on to something.

Jarod took the lead, "Lauren and I make sure we have our signals straight as parents. We make sure we are on the same page with our expectations and how we will handle any discipline. We discuss our approach to the tactics they might use to play us, because they will. That's just part of being a kid. Didn't we do it to our parents? Weren't we just out to get our best deal? By the same token, we never, never use the kids as weapons against each other. That's a short cut to chaos and anarchy as parents."

"Do they ever defy you, or outright disobey?" Marcus inquired.

"Sometimes they do." Lauren admitted. "And there are consequences that Jarod and I have agreed to for various kinds of disobedience, and we follow through."

"Have they ever disappointed you?" Marcus had to ask.

"It has happened." Jarod admitted.

It got quiet.

"Yeah, all the above, Marcus." Jarod reflected. "Then they turn around the next minute and make you so proud you can hardly contain the joy you feel busting out. You look into their faces and realize they are indeed the greatest blessing in life you will ever experience. It is overwhelming." Jarod paused. "I sincerely hope you get to experience it for yourself someday."

Marcus looked at Jarod and up at Lauren who had

placed her right hand on Jarod's left shoulder while standing by the recliner. Jarod reached up with his right hand and laid it on Lauren's as they exchanged glances and a smile that communicated the years of memories they had shared.

"Well, what do you say we get to the game?" Marcus concluded. "Thanks, both of you, for sharing all that."

*   *   *

Admittedly, Marcus was excited that Anna would soon arrive. Marcus inspected his face closely in the bathroom mirror. The vanity lights reflected off his freshly shaved face still damp from rinsing. He dabbed his face with the towel and looked again first at his right profile, then the left. No nicks. *I can't believe I'm acting like a college freshman going out on his first college date.* Marcus approved the inspection, shook his head in self derision, and chuckled under his breath. *No pressure, Marcus. No pressure. OK, Susan, go easy on me.*

Marcus checked his watch for the tenth time in five minutes—4:58. He returned to the student desk and opened his notebook. Before shaving he had written additional insights gleaned from Jarod and Lauren.

Team success = Supervisor's success.

Employees are a lot like kids. (Go figure)
They need attention. They will frustrate
and challenge you. But they will also make
you proud.
Managers must communicate as a group
how they will handle issues among
employees to promote consistency and
overall morale. Can't say that this happens
at M.E. We can do better. Talk to Erin.

Another thought hit Marcus. It was so obvious, he had blown right past it. He added one more principle.

The way we talk to others matters. Tone
of voice, choice of words can cause real
pain. Watch it!

Marcus decided on a starched white shirt to wear with his grey slacks. Then, he wondered if dressing up too much would alert Anna that the kids regarded this as a quasi-date. *On second thought. I'll lose the slacks. Clean pressed jeans will do. Keep the white shirt, but wear it untucked. Roll up the sleeves a couple of turns. Be casual, Marcus.* Marcus dressed, took one last look in the floor length mirror, nodded his approval, and headed downstairs. "No pressure," he reassured himself out loud, slowly letting out a deep breath.

Susan was helping Lauren set the table in the formal dining area. Marcus wondered if Lauren had prepped Anna for the evening. When he entered, everyone tried to sneak a peek without looking like they were putting him through inspection. Everyone, except Andy, who was more excited that his two most favorite people were going to be at dinner with him at the same time. He was negotiating to sit between Coach Flores and Uncle Mark at the dinner table, but Susan informed him that he would be sitting across the table with her and would be able to see both at the same time. Marcus felt on display.

"Lookin' good, Uncle Mark," Susan approved walking up to him enthusiastically hugging him around the waist. "You smell good, too," she whispered before releasing him.

"Thanks," Marcus responded. "Sis, is there anything I can do to help?"

"It's all under control," Lauren replied. "Just relax and enjoy."

Andy had taken up sentry duty at the front door sidelight. "She's here! She's here!" Andy ran gleefully three or four steps toward the kitchen, then back to the front door. "Coach Flores is here, everyone."

Andy didn't wait for the doorbell to ring. He flew out the door and onto the front porch. Lauren was close behind. "Andy, will you escort Coach Flores into the house?" She knew trying to restrain his excitement was futile. Better to go with it. In no time Andy had Coach Flores by the hand and was leading her up the steps onto the porch. Lauren and Jarod had made it to the foyer to greet Anna. Susan was next, and Marcus held back to keep the scene from looking like a receiving line.

"Welcome, Anna," Lauren greeted her. "We are obviously thrilled you could join us. Come in." Lauren took control of Anna from Andy and moved the entourage through the formal section of the house and toward the family room where Marcus had waited.

"You remember my brother, Marcus," Lauren handled the formalities.

"Good to see you again," Marcus nodded.

"Been looking forward to it," Anna offered her hand, with a smile. Marcus held it momentarily and released it.

"Shall we?" Lauren motioned toward the family room.

* * *

The meal and evening were lovely. After the meal, everyone retired to the family room. Andy lavished attention on Anna, and she graciously returned the attention that an adoring nine-year-old boy would remember for months. Anna made sure she addressed both Andy and Susan directly with questions about their interests. Andy had also prepared a drawing of the soccer team playing a match with Coach Flores cheering them on. She thanked Andy with a hug and promised the picture would be displayed in a special place. Susan kept an expectant watch for a hint of Anna's potential interest in Uncle Mark. Eventually, juvenile interest waned, and the adults had the room to themselves. Lauren and Jarod occupied the middle of the leather sofa. Jarod had his right arm around his wife's shoulder. Lauren looked comfortable nestled against his right side. Before Anna arrived, two matching side chairs had been repositioned on either side of the sofa facing each other. Marcus and Anna occupied them. Cozy, but not too intimate.

"Your children are precious," Anna complimented Lauren and Jarod. "Andy is such a dynamo. I'm lucky to get to coach him this year."

Marcus mapped the details of Anna's features in his mind. Her thick dark brown hair framed her oval face from a part slightly left of center, as it tapered around her cheeks and down her back to just below her shoulder blades. Her jaw line was soft, but not delicate, curving into a rounded chin that possessed the slightest of a dimple centered below her full lips. Her straight nose highlighted the perfect symmetry of large almond eyes that invited him in under the archway of sculptured eyebrows. Tonight she wore casual grey slacks and blouse with three-quarter length sleeves. The slacks hugged the curves of her toned hips, but not too tightly. The ivory colored top had the faintest of silver colored threads running vertically through the material that made her shimmer when the light hit them right. She wore delicate silver thread earrings to match the threads in the blouse and a silver cross necklace. A silver thread bracelet on her left wrist matched the earrings. She did not wear a watch or rings. Marcus wished now he had worn the grey slacks.

Marcus spoke. "You rekindled his zeal for soccer, that's for sure. Uh, right Jarod?"

"Right," Jarod echoed.

As much as she was beautiful, Marcus was mesmerized by the energy that radiated from within. Marcus had no words for it.

Marcus continued. "Why did you take on coaching a little boys' soccer team your first year of being in a law practice? I would think your job would demand all your time."

"It is demanding, but for me, I find it beneficial to have something completely outside work that demands my mental and physical attention. That's why I liked playing soccer so much as a little girl and especially in college. I think the physical energy kept me mentally sharp as well," Anna explained.

"Why a little boys' team, and not a girls'?" Marcus asked.

"Simple. There was a last minute opening to coach this team, and I was available and willing," Anna answered. "It was fate, I guess, because I have just fallen in love with these little guys. I'm the baby sister of two older brothers who taught me to love soccer. Now I have twelve little brothers to do the same for."

"You obviously have them captivated," Marcus said.

"Well, it's my first attempt at coaching. I'm sure I'll make my share of mistakes." Anna glanced at Jarod and Lauren. "I just focus on helping the boys fall in love with the game first, and to help them find their own talents in the game." Anna said.

"What about the pressure to win?" Marcus wanted to know.

"I know many coaches emphasize winning." Anna shifted in her chair. "I played competitive soccer since I was eleven, and believe me I understand the competitive spirit to win. I also learned along the way that it depends how you define win. There were many times we didn't outscore an opponent that was better than we were, but you would never convince me that we didn't win if we had given it all on the field and competed until the final whistle." Anna could see Marcus was dialed in to what she was saying. "When a better opponent elevates you to perform at a higher level, you're a winner. Don't you think?"

Marcus was nodding his head in agreement, "Been there. I know exactly what you mean."

Anna went on, "I feel at this age winning will take care of itself, and there will be plenty of time to focus on winning as the boys mature as players."

"I think I had forgotten how important that perspective is," Marcus added. "Sometimes we expect too much too soon."

Lauren took over, "Anna, may I ask how do you stay in such wonderful shape? Don't tell me you run five miles every morning before work."

Anna laughed, "Well, truth is I do work out regularly, because I always have. Habit, I guess. More than that, I live by a philosophy of, 'good in, good out,' which just reminds me to be good to myself in the way I choose to live."

Marcus was impressed, and eager to agree. "We would all do well to adopt that philosophy."

Anna continued, "It reminds me, I had a friend in high school who loved the movie *Bill and Ted's Excellent Adventure.*" She giggled, "He kept repeating a line from it, something like, 'party on, dude, and be excellent to each other.' That stuck with me, and I got to thinking, why not? Why shouldn't we be excellent to each other and to ourselves, and not take ourselves so seriously all the time? I decided I'd try to live that philosophy, and it seems to work for me."

Anna had questions, too. "Marcus, Lauren tells me you were recently promoted. Congratulations. I trust that is going well."

Marcus chose his words. "The learning curve is steeper than I thought it would be, but I'm starting to get the picture of how to handle it."

"I'm sure you'll do well," Anna assured.

"Marcus is an athlete, too," Lauren inserted herself again into the conversation.

"Yeah? Tell me more," Anna was interested and looked at Marcus for a response.

"Cross country," Marcus downplayed it without going into detail.

"Little brother, you are much too modest," Lauren was eager to brag on him. "Marcus was on a state runner up team in high school, and he ran on scholarship in college," she added proudly.

"Maybe on your next trip up we can take a run together," Anna offered.

"I'll have to get back in better shape to keep up with you," Marcus grinned, a little embarrassed.

"It begins with the first step," Anna replied.

"Do you believe in serendipity?" Marcus asked impulsively, forgetting that Lauren and Jarod were sitting nearby.

"I believe the world is full of surprises and unexpected events," Anna replied. "Isn't that what makes life interesting? Every moment and every encounter is brimming with possibilities. Don't you agree?"

"Yes." Marcus nodded looking deeply into Anna's eyes. "Yes, I do."

There was a pause.

Anna broke the silence. "Well, Lauren and Jarod, thank you for a lovely evening. If Andy isn't asleep yet, I'd also like to say good night and thank him again for the picture he drew for me." Anna moved to stand.

Everyone took the cue. Jarod walked to the children's wing of the downstairs and called for them to come say good night to Coach Flores. Andy ran to hug her. Susan said good night then turned and glanced up at Marcus, grinned and winked.

The grown ups walked Anna toward the front door. Marcus stepped onto the front porch with her. She turned and smiled and handed him a business card. "Call me," she said. "Anytime."

"Will do," Marcus replied. Anna walked to her car, turned and smiled at Marcus before sliding into the driver's seat. Marcus waited until she pulled out of the drive before glancing at the card. Across the top she had written her personal cell number, and under it she added,

"Next first step?"

8
Next first step

Serendipity is an interesting sounding word, Marcus thought as he unbuttoned his shirt, slipped out of it, and tossed it over the back of the chair. Marcus whispered it, "Serendipity." It had a happy-go-lucky ring to it sort of like zippity-doo-dah, zippity-aye. Like Anna said, life is full of surprises. This weekend had turned out to be one. Friday morning Marcus was writhing in anxiety; now, by Sunday night, he felt like his whole life was about to change thanks to one surprise after another. Andy, Susan, Jarod, Lauren, Jeannie, Johnny, Kelly, Nick, the labyrinth, and, of course, Anna—one at a time and each in his or her own way had provided a tidbit of information, an insight, or advice that, when taken as a whole, showed Marcus the way back from his disaster with Erin Friday morning.

While Anna's conversation was still fresh, he needed to summarize a couple of additional principles he had picked up. He opened the notebook and wrote.

Be excellent to others and to yourself.
good in — good out.
Winning can be defined a number of ways.
Don't pass up on opportunities, even if
they seem counter to our expectations
(i.e. a woman coaching a boys' soccer
team. The opportunity presented itself
unexpectedly, and Anna was open enough to
take it.) Like Andy said, all that counts is
that she's good at it. Performance speaks.
And to go with that — welcome the
unexpected. change challenges you to
rethink, re-evaluate, and grow.
Be authentic. Anna surprised me by being
so transparent with her thoughts. I think
she is as she seems to be. Natural.
Sincere.

Marcus read back over his notes. It was late, and
he just wanted to rest and reflect. Monday would be a
day of action. He would begin by summarizing and
organizing the insights and ideas he had developed
since Friday, and formulate the conversation he intended to have with Erin as soon as he returned to

work. *Yes, Jeannie Irwin. It is a new day.* Marcus closed his eyes as he lay on top of the covers. He felt no tension whatsoever.

*   *   *

A hazelnut aroma wafted into Marcus's room greeting him as he stirred from his sleep. *Jarod's up*, was his first thought. Even though the kids were out of school today, it was another workday for Jarod. *Kids are probably sleeping in. Think I'll join Jarod and say bye before he gets out the door.* The digital alarm clock told Marcus it was 6:07. *About the time I usually get up anyway. First step, Marcus. Get moving.*

Jarod stood at the kitchen bar sipping coffee and scanning the local newspaper's dot-com version on the iPad when Marcus entered the kitchen. Jarod looked up from his reading, "Morning. Thought I'd better get my time on the iPad before Andy gets hold of it."

"What's going on in the world?" Marcus asked as he filled the tea kettle.

"Not much, really. Usual politics and sports. Oh, here's something." Jarod acted surprised by a headline. He continued without looking up, " Listen to this. Visiting wind engineer electrified by local soccer coach," Jarod exclaimed, intoning dramatically as if he were reading a headline.

"Come on, Jarod." Marcus begged off. "It wasn't like that at all."

"Ga-a-a-awd, Marcus." Jarod couldn't contain his laughter as he spoke, "If you could only have sat where I sat and watched your face."

"There are forces at work, and we are merely accidental accomplices," Lauren made her entrance. "Morning, little brother." She took a step over to Marcus and kissed him on the cheek, turned to Jarod and exchanged a good morning kiss.

"So, Jarod said I was taken by Anna." Marcus said.

"Understatement. More like schmockered silly." Lauren replied.

"*Schmockered?* That's not a word." Marcus said. "You just made that up."

"Yeah, but it fits." Lauren poured coffee for herself and sipped, "Did you get her phone number?"

"Um, she gave it to me outside." Marcus admitted.

"Yep. Schmockered." Lauren headed for the family room. The tea kettle whistled. "Water's boiling. And, you're wearing that silly 'What?' grin."

Marcus turned off the burner under the kettle, retrieved a tea bag, and prepped the cup. *She's right.* Marcus thought. *Forces at work. Serendipity. Hey, there's another idea I hadn't thought of 'till now. Forces that are at work around us. Independent forces of nature that affect us in various ways. Gravity, magnetism, motion, energy. I studied all those in college and count on their consistency every day. Maybe there are others? Motivation could be like that. Love? Passions? Fear?* "Hmmmmm." Marcus sounded as he poured water over the tea bag.

"Marcus," Lauren called from the family room where she sat next to Jarod sharing morning coffee. "Want me to fix you some breakfast? I'm gonna make us some pancakes."

"Why don't you two just enjoy your coffee and let me fix breakfast. I'm not planning to start back home until after lunch anyway." Marcus felt a great day coming on.

* * *

The kids were out of school for a teacher in-service day. That was the main reason Marcus had extended his stay an extra day. "Uncle Mark?" Andy appeared at the table on the veranda where Marcus had his notebook opened in front of him and his laptop out, ready to power up. "Will you play some video games with me before you go back home today?" he asked.

"Sure, sport. I'd love to. I just need about thirty minutes to finish this up. OK?" Marcus answered.

"Super!" Andy exclaimed and headed back in, just about bumping into Susan as she came out the back door.

"Watch it, Andy." Susan warned, dodging her excited brother. She was wide-eyed and grinning ear-to-ear as she approached the table. "Mom said you and

Coach Flores seemed to like each other a lot," Susan could hardly wait to hear Marcus's spin, exuberant at the prospect of adolescent gossip.

"Just try to convince me that you and your mom didn't have an ulterior motive for inviting Coach Flores to dinner." Marcus stated.

"It's just the way we noticed you watching her at Andy's soccer match, and we thought wel-l-l-l, why not? But it was mostly my idea. Mom just went along." Susan confessed. "Mom called her about it while you were out walking Saturday afternoon."

"You two are sooooo bad." Marcus teased.

"You'll thank us later." Susan grinned. She hurried a peck-of-a kiss on his right cheek and headed back indoors. She turned and looked back at Marcus as she reached the door, "I'm right. I know it."

Marcus returned to his work. His phone chimed, and he looked down at the text message it alerted:

"appreciate change of mind. c u n morning."

"Good." He said out loud to himself. It was from Brad. Earlier, Marcus had sent a text saying that, on second thought, he would be happy to review Brad's report with him when he returned Tuesday morning. "A first step taken."

Marcus scanned the pages of notes he had rewritten this morning. He was ready to put them in a more finished form and decided to type them into his laptop. He hoped it would make as much sense to Erin when he talked to her as it made to him now. He had already called her an hour earlier, telling her he had done a lot of reflecting and thinking about what she said Friday, and he wanted to visit with her at seven-thirty in the morning if possible. She agreed, and suggested they meet at the coffee shop nearby where they would not be interrupted and where they might feel more relaxed. The meeting was set. He was ready. "First steps. Begin." Marcus started typing.

Premise: People are naturally motivated to "win" whatever that means to them individually.

Application: I believe people come to work everyday wanting to do their best at something they enjoy and know how to do. They want to feel good about themselves and the work they do and be appreciated for it.

Personal takeaway: It's my duty as a supervisor to help make that happen for those who are entrusted to my care.

SUPERVISING IS A LIFESTYLE, NOT A JOB.
AS A SUPERVISOR, MY FOCUS IS TO CREATE VALUE FOR EVERYONE INVOLVED.
SUPERVISING IS A TRUST RELATIONSHIP.
MY TEAM IS ENTRUSTED TO ME, AND I AM BEING TRUSTED TO LEAD THEM.
SUCCESSFUL SUPERVISORS MUST BE:

1. PEOPLE ORIENTED
2. CLEAR MINDED
3. PERFORMANCE DRIVEN

PEOPLE ORIENTED means realizing that everyone is just trying to do his or her best to make it in the world. To each person, everything is personal. The way we talk and act toward each other has a personal impact. Everyone matters. Every human being is equally valuable without exception. Different people have different needs, wants, and values, and act according to them. We need each other, and live in a network of relationships.

CLEAR MINDED means as a leader I must be absolutely clear about what we are wanting to accomplish as a team and communicate it directly and often. I must set the standard for quality and behavior and hold myself accountable for it. I must clearly communicate what "win" means as it relates to our mission and assignment. I must be certain of my values and beliefs, because they come across in the way I act and treat others.

PERFORMANCE DRIVEN means I should expect people to perform, and I must communicate in my daily supervising how they are doing. It's my job to coach and help my staff improve according to their talents and natural abilities. If they see me doing my job well, they will be more motivated to want to do theirs well. Speak affirmatively and kindly. The way we talk to others can spur cooperation and performance, or resentment and resistance.

There are some principles that both embody and underlie

the preceding comments. These principles can be applied to many life situations:

1. **We live in a network of relationships.** We are all connected. Everything gets done through networks of relationships. When people connect, the possibilities are endless. Each of us is personally responsible for the quality of our relationships.

2. **Everything is personal, and everyone matters.** The only reality you know is the self you are, defined by your beliefs, experiences, relationships, and dreams. Your work is a manifestation of your innermost self, springing from the depths of your creative mind and spirit. Every human is equally valuable without exception.

3. **Everyone seeks personal meaning.** A person's search for meaning is the most powerful hunger in the human spirit. We want to be important and to have made a difference in our lives.

4. **Everyone is personally accountable.** How you live your life is your choice, and you are responsible for it. Live mindfully in the present. Take affirmative action now.

5. **Be excellent to yourself and to others.** Live excellently. Be honest, self-aware, and authentic—no games, no masks. Tell your truth kindly. Filling yourself with goodness will drive out the bad.

6. **Change and diversity are life giving processes.** It's the unusual, unexpected, and odd that surprise us, thrill us, and renew us. Welcome it, and be stimulated by it.

7. **Trust the force.** The pure energy of creativity, motivation,

love, and passion are naturally available to work in us and for us in every aspect of our life. Go with it.

Marcus paused and read back over what he had just typed. "It's a good first step," he said with a sense of satisfaction, "a good first step." He placed the cursor over the menu bar and clicked, "file" then "save" and typed "firststep" and clicked the "save" button.

"Ready yet, Uncle Mark?" Andy stuck his head out the back door. He had been watching the clock.

Andy's computer game skills testified to his practice and precocious nature. It was all Marcus could do to hold his own against him. Susan flittered in and out of the family room while they played. She obviously had something on her mind.

"Susan, did you want me for something?" Marcus finally asked while Andy reset for another game.

"I was wondering if you were coming back up for Halloween like you did last year?" She sounded a bit conniving the way she asked. "Mom wanted me to ask, cause we'd need to make another costume."

"I think I might be able to. It depends. There's this project we are trying to complete at work. And then, I'll have to double check my social calendar." Marcus answered a bit facetiously.

"I'll take that as a yes," Susan said then turned and hollered as she left the room, "Mommmm. Uncle Mark said yes."

"I guess that settles it." He said to Andy. "I have time for one more game, then I've gotta get ready to head back to Tulsa."

*   *   *

The drive back for Marcus was much more relaxed than the drive up Friday afternoon. He rehearsed the meeting he expected to have with Erin in the morning. He thought of what he needed to do to heal the unspoken rift with his team. He went over the points he had collected in the notebook and how much sense they made to him.

He was struck that he found so many parallels between the individual stories he came across during the weekend and how they applied to supervising, or at least prompted ideas that he could apply to his situation. He had never thought about the similarities of supervising and being a parent, but now they struck him as so obvious. The more he reflected on Lauren and Jarod, the more he realized that, just like parents, it's the supervisor who is responsible for the care and welfare of his work group—or hers, as the case might be. Lauren was right. There had been a fundamental life change since he accepted the position. He just had not recognized it and lived up to it. He would change that. He wondered what would happen to Jeannie and if he should try to stay in contact some way. And then, there was AnnaMarie Flores.

Maybe there were more changes in the wind.

*   *   *

Marcus arrived at the coffee shop shortly after seven o'clock Tuesday morning and took a table in the back corner where he and Erin could talk undisturbed. He sipped tea and ate a croissant while he reviewed his points. He was nervous and excited as he kept his eyes on the front door.

Erin arrived at 7:25 by Marcus's watch. He stepped up to greet her and intercepted her just as she arrived at the order counter. "Here, Erin, let me treat you," Marcus offered. She accepted, and Marcus also ordered another tea.

"I was glad to hear from you yesterday morning. I'm looking forward to hearing the details of what you said you wanted to share," Erin sounded pleased. They took their drinks and went to the table.

"Erin, let me just say it was an eye-opening weekend that I did not expect," Marcus began. "As I drove up to my sister's Friday afternoon, I was just hoping that you would see that I was right and that you had not made a mistake promoting me. Then, things started happening, and I began meeting people who, without saying a word about business or management, helped me see my circumstances in a very different way. I want to share with you the substance of what they unknowingly taught me, and how I think I can apply it and live up to the confidence you placed in me last March."

Marcus put a copy of the file he had typed Monday morning in front of Erin and explained his conclusions and observations. She listened without interrupting and read through the points as Marcus went over them. He briefly mentioned his sister and brother-in-law, niece and nephew, Jeannie and her family, and Anna and the contributions each had made to his new understanding.

"I must say, Marcus, when you left the office Friday I never thought I would see you grow up so quickly in your thinking. I'm so glad you figured all this out on your own," Erin beamed with relief.

"Honestly, I had many teachers over the weekend. Accidental accomplices in my turn around. Which made me realize that I could use a mentor as I learn how to become the kind of supervisor everyone wants to work with instead of run away from. Will you help me identify one?" Marcus asked hopefully.

"I would be thrilled to. Several come to mind right away, and I'll get started on helping you with that," Erin promised. "In the meantime, Marcus, I'm confident you will turn this around. Brad told me yesterday you plan to meet him this morning. I think that's a good first step. Are there any other first steps you plan to take to answer some of the concerns I expressed Friday?"

"Absolutely," Marcus replied and went down his notes of the things he planned to do for each of the individuals on his team.

Erin listened intently while Marcus explained his strategy. "Marcus, I don't know what all happened at your sister's over the weekend, but I'm confident that you will deliver on everything you said this morning. I can tell you are sincere about the changes you want to make. If you follow through like I think you can, you will become an excellent supervisor and leader for your team and in this company," Erin said. "I knew I was right about you."

"I appreciate your faith in me, Erin. Thank you for another chance," Marcus said.

"Obviously, southwest Missouri agrees with you, Marcus," Erin changed the subject. "You are so much more at ease today than at any time since your promotion."

"Some good things happened to me. It's been a very interesting three days," Marcus said.

Erin, picked up her phone, tapped the screen several times. "Would this have anything to do with it?" She turned the screen toward Marcus. There was a photo of AnnaMarie Flores smiling back at him. "My cousin is giddy over some guy from Tulsa named Marcus that she met over the weekend. He's the uncle of one of her nine-year-old soccer players. She thought I might know you," Erin glanced up at Marcus who could not contain his surprise. "I told her she had an eye for quality."

Marcus broke into a wide smile and asked, "Do you believe in serendipity?"

Performance review:
Three months later

Marcus's phone chimed about the same time he sat down at his desk in the mesh ergonomic office chair. Anna's text inquired,

"had ur meeting yet?"

Marcus tapped the favorites tab with his thumb, then Anna's name. Her photo popped up on the screen with the caption, "Calling Anna."

The ring tone sounded only once. "How did it go? I want to hear all about it," Anna asked eagerly.

"Well, hello to you, too," Marcus chuckled. "Everything went very well. Everyone was pleased with how much the team has improved so soon, and they were very complimentary of my progress as a supervisor. I'll give you all the details when I call tonight," Marcus reported. "I feel really great about it all."

"That's soooo wonderful to hear. I expected no less. Nine-thirty as usual?" Anna asked.

"Nine-thirty as usual," Marcus confirmed.

"Still treating your team to lunch today?" Anna continued.

"Absolutely. We'll be leaving in a few minutes. I'm glad I have good news to share with them," Marcus added.

Marcus and Anna exchanged good-byes as Marcus glanced at a photo taken of them on what they considered their first official date—dressed as vampires at the community center Halloween party. Of course, Andy stood in front of them beaming in his fake fang teeth giving his most horrifying vampire smile.

Susan's proclamation on the veranda that she was right about him and Anna seemed prophetic, looking back on it. They seemed a very natural couple, and Marcus was happy about the direction and pace of their growing relationship.

Marcus swiveled and looked out over the park across the street from Millennium Energy's campus. The final patches of a January snow glistened in the midday sun. The morning meeting with Erin Morales, his supervising project manager, and Gerald Donovan, vice president of research and development, had gone even better than expected. Though confident, Marcus had been nervous all week as he prepared for the review. He had made some big promises to Erin back in October about how he could turn his performance around, and he had felt good about his results. He had diligently applied the principles he had identified on that weekend at his sister's home. Marcus reflected back on the specific steps he had taken.

- He met with his managers to make sure he was clear about their expectations for his project and how the project related to the mission of the company.

- He met with his team the afternoon of his return and apologized for his behavior. If he had committed transgressions in public, he apologized in public. He discussed the focus of their project and asked for their ideas of how he could serve them better as a supervisor. He expressed his confidence in their talent.

- He met with each team member individually and reiterated what he had said in the team meeting. He apologized privately for specific things he could remember that he had done to offend and asked if there were other situations he needed to make right.

- He spent more time working with them individually and as a group instead of sequestering himself in his office. He changed his focus from doing work, to supervising his team and managing their work processes.

- He made himself consciously aware of his tone of voice and mannerisms to make sure he looked and sounded more supportive.

- He worked on being clear and thorough in the way he set performance expectations and discussed whether expectations were in line with team capabilities. He looked for successes.

- He discussed with each individual his or her talents and interests and how to help develop them to the fullest. He also challenged them to identify and exploit latent talents that he saw in them.

It took daily concentration and discipline from Marcus, and all his efforts paid off. The team developed some breakthrough technology on their project, allowing the company to compete for the investors they sought. Marcus could see the group bond as they challenged each other for new ideas. Everyone wanted to win.

Marcus began meeting with a mentor. Erin had matched him up with Elliot Sloan, a vice president in the natural gas production division of their parent company. They met at least every other week to discuss progress. His mentor also was introducing him to other managers who could be role models. His professional network was growing.

Marcus glanced down at the photo of him and Anna again as his thoughts drifted back to the personal payoff that he couldn't wait to share with Anna, which had come from Gerald. *"Marcus, Erin shared the first steps file with me that you gave her last October. I've watched your progress and compared it to what you wrote about supervision being a lifestyle. I thought your three points about managers being people oriented, clear minded, and performance driven were especially pertinent. I was wondering if you would be willing to present your ideas at our management leadership retreat this spring. What do you say?"*

Marcus beamed, "It would be my honor. Thank you for your confidence."

Gerald smiled at Erin from the corner of his eyes and offered his hand across the table to Marcus, "It's settled then. I believe this will be a great first step."

A tap on the glass wall of Marcus's office brought him back into the moment. Brad was signaling that it was time for lunch. Marcus's phone chimed again. He glanced at the message.

"TOY. THX for introducing me to Anna. needed a big sis. LOLO. it's a new day."

A sensation of happiness and optimism warmed Marcus. He spoke out loud to himself as he pocketed the phone and reached for his coat, "Yes, it is, Jeannie Irwin. Yes, it is."

TO BE CONTINUED

The MANAGEMENT *You*™ philosophy for **INPOWERED** managers

"Management at all levels is a trust relationship dedicated to creating value for all stakeholders. To do so, **INPOWERED** managers must be:

1. People- oriented
2. Clear-minded, and
3. Performance-driven

Because, people come to work every day motivated to do the best job they know how, at something they enjoy, to feel good about who they are, and be appreciated for it."

~Garland C. McWatters, Jr.

Author's Afterword

The principles of managing and leading that Marcus Winn discovered and applied to his situation comprise the core values of my personal management philosophy. The file that he typed and presented to Erin Morales verbalizes what I believe to be the essence of establishing what I call, **INPOWERED** workplaces.

My quest is to unleash heart and soul in the workplace again. Goodness is in our DNA. I believe that people go to work everyday wanting to do the best they know how, at something they enjoy, to feel good about who they are, and be appreciated for it. They are looking for the way.

As Jeannie asked Marcus on that lakeside bench, *"Aren't we all just trying to make it, Marcus? Look around! People are just trying to make it, and make sense of it all in their own way."*

A new generation is stepping up to take its place in the world. I've never been more optimistic about our future. Marcus Winn, and aspiring leaders like him, men and women, have a lot to teach us from what they are learning.

It's a new day, and a big first step.

Acknowledgments

This Marcus Winn story is possible because of the many who, after taking my leadership and management courses, encouraged me to write a business book. You **INCOURAGE** my spirit.

To those who **INLIGHTEN** my mind and **INLIVEN** my heart, your contributions are priceless. Among those who contributed to this book in various ways are: Lynda Atkins, Billy Bailey, Rick Bedlion, Danny Burgin, Larry Fisher, Maura Schreier-Fleming, Cindy Friedemann, Sabrina Froehlich, Shelia Littleton, Daryll McCarthy, Jason McWatters, Jane McWatters, Denise Nilssen, Marie Piet, Brian Perryman, Randy Rogers, LaShon Ross, Lorinda Schrammel, and Ron Walton. There are several who have been fans and true believers of my work since the beginning. They deserve particular mention: Denise Nilssen, Lorinda Schrammel, Jack Pryor, and Ken King. My good friend, Peter Vail, and I spent hours together over the years discussing leadership and management. Much of what I have learned was filtered through those conversations.

To those who have **INLARGED** my expectations of living, I hope this book is testimony to your influence. I especially thank mentors, Bruce and Jim, for seeing the possibilities in me and believing in your hunches.

The Author

Garland C. McWatters, Jr. is a storyteller, author, and trainer. His passion is to create **INPOWERING** workplaces populated by **INPOWERED** leaders and contributors.

Garland has enjoyed a variety of professional experiences including broadcasting, journalism, public relations, education, sales, and the ministry. Since 1994, Garland has written and presented training programs in management, leadership, and work process. He has worked from the shop floor to the corporate boardroom in a variety of businesses and organizations of all sizes. His work has taken him to manufacturing of all kinds; information technology; local, county, and state government; financial institutions; insurance; distribution centers; educational institutions; public relations; marketing, and aviation.

Learn more about Garland and his work at his business website: www.managementyou.com

Made in the USA
Charleston, SC
23 March 2013